6813

929.9
Egg
c.5   Eggenberger, David

                Flags of the U.S.A.

FLAGS OF THE U.S.A.

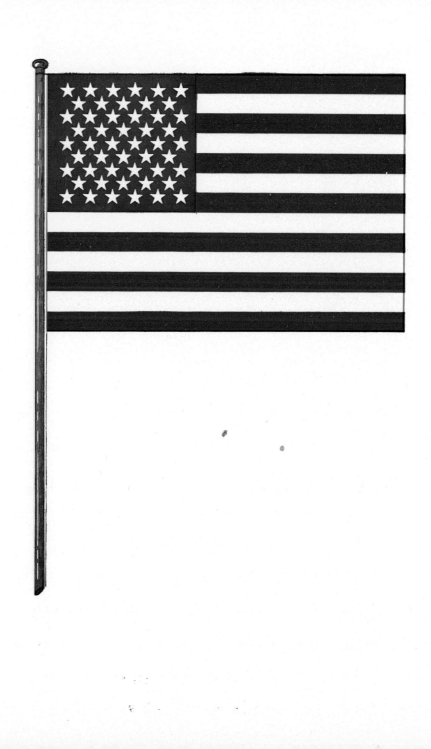

David Eggenberger

★ FLAGS
★
★ OF THE
★
★ U.S.A.
★

Enlarged Edition

Thomas Y. Crowell Company
New York ★★★★ *Established 1834*

The author is grateful for help from many sources, particularly the Smithsonian Institution, Library of Congress, West Point Museum, John Carter Brown Library, and Pennsylvania Society of Sons of the Revolution.

The photographs on pages 170 and 171 are reproduced by courtesy of the United Nations and H. Armstrong Roberts, respectively.

★ DESIGNED BY NANCY H. DALE

★ *Manufactured in the United States of America*

★ LIBRARY OF CONGRESS CATALOG CARD NO. 64-12115

★   7 8 9 10

★ ★ ★ ★ ★

★ ★ ★ ★ ★

★ ★ ★ ★ ★

CONTENTS ▮▮▮▮▮▮▮▮▮▮▮▮▮▮▮▮▮▮▮

▮▮▮▮▮▮▮▮▮▮▮▮▮▮▮▮▮▮▮▮▮▮▮▮▮▮▮▮▮▮▮▮▮▮▮

CHAPTER 1

★ ★ ★ ★ ★

★ ★ ★ ★ ★

THE BRITISH UNION FLAG OUTLASTS ITS RIVALS

It is the morning of September 13, 1759, chill and dark. Two hostile armies are drawn up on a mile-wide plateau outside the French city of Quebec. Across the rain-soaked grass the blue-and-white uniformed troops of French King Louis XV face the red-coated army of England's George II. Both forces are well-trained regulars, brightly attired and battle hardened. Skirmishers and sharpshooters fire sporadically as the French form for attack. Six hundred paces to the west, the British are rigidly aligned, waiting to receive the blow.

At ten o'clock, the French begin their advance, shouting and firing as they move steadily forward. British lines are motionless except for the closing of

The British Union Flag Outlasts Its Rivals ★ 1

ranks over fallen comrades. The French attackers press on until only forty paces separate the combatants. Then the British act. With parade-ground precision every redcoat raises his musket and, on command, they pour a terrible volley into the foe. And another! The concentrated fire cuts the French lines to pieces. A savage bayonet charge, and the French army flees in confusion.

In those few minutes the battle of Quebec was won, and, for all practical purposes, the French and Indian War as well. More important, on the Plains of Abraham that autumn morning a momentous and far-reaching issue was decided—a continent was won and lost. French power in North America was forever ended. The British Union flew unchallenged from Canada to Georgia and—except for the French city of New Orleans —from the Atlantic to the Mississippi.

What was this British flag that had outlasted its rivals to win domination over a continent? The flag that was the first to unite the future United States under one banner?

Actually it was two flags—a red cross on white and a white cross on blue—combined into a stately red, white, and blue banner called the Union Flag, or (incorrectly) the King's Colors. The original flag of England, adopted during the Crusades, was the red cross of St. George. In 1603, when James VI of Scotland became also James I of England, a new flag seemed indicated. English sailors refused to dip their colors to the national flag of Scotland—the white cross of St. Andrew on a blue field. The Scots were equally scornful of St. George's cross. James accordingly ordered his

2 ★ *Flags of the U.S.A.*

heralds to design a new flag, and the result was the Union Flag, adopted in 1606. To maintain national identities, both the Scots and the English were allowed to fly their ancient banners as secondary flags on the foremasts of ships. The Union had to be hoisted at the main.

As a further aid in identifying ships during battle a new English flag came into use in the middle 1600's. This was a bright red banner charged with the union device in the canton (or rectangular division in the upper corner next the staff). Following the Act of Union between England, Scotland, and Wales in 1707 this flag became Great Britain's Red Ensign, or merchant flag, later called the Meteor Flag.[1] In America the Red Ensign became the flag of the Colonists on both land and sea—a symbol of authority unquestioned until the Revolution. It was also the flag of British land forces, for after 1634 use of the Union Flag was forbidden to all but the Royal Navy. As the official emblem of the military, the Red Ensign was proudly, often arrogantly, flown throughout the Colonies until that fateful day at Yorktown when the British Army band played "The World Turned Upside Down."

The uniting of North America under one flag had been a long, laborious project. A colorful variety of European banners had appeared on the continent from

[1] A name popularized by the Scottish poet Thomas Campbell in his "Ye Mariners of England" (1801):
> The meteor flag of England
> Shall yet terrific burn,
> Till danger's troubled night depart,
> And the star of peace return.

The British Union Flag Outlasts Its Rivals ★ 3

time to time. Some of them were seen only fleetingly and never appeared again; others were worthy challengers, subdued only after stubborn resistance.

The first European flag to arrive in the New World was also the first to leave. It was the banner of the Vikings—a black raven with outspread wings on a white field—carried across the Atlantic by the daring Leif Ericson about A.D. 1000. During the next few years Leif's brother Thorvald led other Norse expeditions to what they called Vinland (variously located from Labrador to as far south as Virginia). The Vikings, however, made no lasting settlement. Their interest in the West died out with the passing of the years. America had to be discovered all over again.

The rediscovery did not take place until almost five hundred years later. But this time it was for good. The discoverer was Christopher Columbus; the date, a familiar one to all, 1492; and the flag, the quartered banner of Castile and León—a castle in the first and fourth quarters, a lion in the second and third. Columbus also carried a personal standard featuring a green Latin cross between the letters "F" and "Y" for his sponsors King Ferdinand and Queen Ysabella (Isabella) of Spain.

Throughout the next century the Spanish flag represented the greatest European power in the New World. But Spain dissipated much of its energy in quest of golden fantasies—the Fountain of Youth, the Seven Cities of Cibola, Quivira, El Dorado. Only one of these searches led to the establishment of the Spanish flag at North America's front door. In 1513 Juan Ponce de León landed in Florida and claimed that land for Ferdinand V. This claim was cashed in 1565 when the cruel Pedro Menéndez de Avilés drove out French Huguenot squatters and founded St. Augustine. The Spanish flag flew here for almost two hundred years but its hold was perilous, its existence constantly threatened. Finally, in 1763, the British Union became the flag of Florida—the Spanish House of Bourbon had drawn a loser's chair at the Peace of Paris conference table.

The Spanish flag flew in Louisiana Territory from 1762 to 1803, and reappeared over Florida from 1783 to 1821, but by then Spain had been reduced to a second-rate power, a satellite of France. Similarly, the Spanish banner in the Southwest and the Russian emblem on the Pacific coast (after 1741) represented forces confined to the back door of the continent. The struggle for power in North America would be decided in the East. On the Plains of Abraham and later on a swampy peninsula in Virginia.

While the Spanish were occupied with their will-o'-the-wisp adventures, two muscular European nations began their long and bitter contest for control of North America. In two voyages, 1497 and 1498, a Genoese merchant-sailor, John Cabot, explored the north Atlantic coast, claiming it for Henry VII of England. Cabot carried the red cross of St. George for his flag—a design that still lives today in two flags of the Western hemisphere, Canada and Hawaii. The French made their move in 1534. Flying the ancient fleur-de-lis banner of France, sturdy Jacques Cartier of France sailed into the Gulf of St. Lawrence and claimed half a continent for Francis I.

In the next century both nations solidified and strengthened their claims in the New World. English settlers raised their flag over colonies founded at Jamestown (1607), Plymouth (1620), and elsewhere along the Atlantic coast. From the New France settlements at Quebec (1608) and Montreal (1642) French trappers and traders carried the fleur-de-lis banner west and south from the St. Lawrence, staking out a sickle-shaped empire that stretched as far as New Orleans by 1718.

Meanwhile the flag of another European nation was hoisted in the New World. In 1609 an Englishman, Henry Hudson, sailed into what is now New York harbor with the orange, white, and blue banner of the Netherlands flying from the mainmast of the *Half Moon*. On the white stripe were the letters A.O.C. for Hudson's sponsor, the Algemeene Oost-Indische Compagnie, or United East India Company of Amsterdam. The A.O.C. charter—and flag—expired before any permanent settlement could be effected. A new company and a new flag achieved better results. In 1623 the Geoctrooyerd West-Indische Compagnie (Chartered West India Company) founded the province of New Netherland along the Hudson River. This company also flew the Netherlands banner but with its G.W.C. initials in the white stripe.

Three years later the company's director general, Peter Minuit, made one of the best buys in real estate history. For sixty guilders (twenty-four dollars) he bought Manhattan Island from the Canarsie Indians and there he founded New Amsterdam. (The colorful director general was actually not as shrewd as his reputation would have it, for the real owners, the Manhatoes, had to be reimbursed later.)

Peter Minuit also had a hand in bringing to America the last challenger for control of the continent—Sweden. After leaving the Dutch colony in 1628 Minuit helped organize the New Sweden Company and ten years later he founded a Swedish settlement on the Delaware River (within the present limits of Wilmington, Delaware). Minuit's flag was now the historic banner of Sweden— a gold cross on a blue field.

The new colony attained such a prosperity that it attracted the covetous eye of the New Netherland governor, the strong-minded Peter Stuyvesant. ("We derive our authority from God and the Company and not from a few ignorant subjects.") In 1655 Stuyvesant marched his troops into New Sweden, hauled down the Swedish flag, and ran up the newly adopted Netherlands flag of red, white, and blue. Sweden's bid for America had been stamped out.

The stamping shoe was soon on the other foot. In 1664 an English task force of four frigates forced Stuyvesant to surrender New Netherland to Charles II. The Dutch flag came down in New Amsterdam and the British Union went up in New York.

Only two European flags now remained in active contention for possession of North America, the English and the French. Their antagonism was sharp and bitter. From 1689 to 1748 hostility between England and France flashed into three inconclusive wars followed by three equally inconclusive peace treaties. (The American phases of these conflicts were called: King William's War, Queen Anne's War, and King George's War.) The fourth and decisive conflict was the French and Indian War, with its climax at Quebec. It shattered French power in America and expelled the fleur-de-lis banner from the continent.[2]

During the long years of Anglo-French warfare American Colonial levies and British regulars had fought side by side, and under the same flag. This mutual sharing of the hardships and hazards of war produced a deep respect for the Union Flag of the Royal Navy and the Meteor Flag of the English land forces. The British flag meant arms, money, and men to fight the French and their Indian allies. It represented stable government, benevolent protection, a common heritage. And it was the proud symbol of the motherland. The crosses of St. George and St. Andrew had reached a new high of popularity on the continent of North America. Who dared question their authority?

---

[2] When French forces returned as allies of the Americans during the Revolution, Admiral de Grasse flew a white flag—the *pavillon blanc*—and each regiment carried a white colonel's flag plus its own varicolored company banners.

CHAPTER 2

★ ★ ★ ★ ★

★ ★ ★ ★ ★

PINE TREES, RATTLE-SNAKES, AND REVOLUTION

What was unthinkable in 1763 became inevitable in 1776. During those thirteen convulsive years the British flag in America changed from a symbol of affection and benevolence to an emblem of hatred and oppression.

At the same time, its inviolate position was being challenged by a score or more of impudent banners devised by Colonial "rebels" to express their aims and aspirations. The high determination behind these heraldic efforts and the critical events associated with the actual banners constitute one of the proudest and most colorful chapters in the history of the nation.

Until the opening of the Revolutionary period there had been few occasions for the Colonists to alter existing flags or to devise new ones. The first venture in American heraldry was a hasty improvisation. In 1634 a Puritan leader, John Endicott, had rashly hauled down the English Red Ensign from a flagstaff in Naumkeag (now Salem) and with his sword cut out the canton containing the cross of St. George. The cross, it seems, was one of the "idolatrous remnants of popery" he was determined to purge from the Anglican church. Fearful of the consequences of Endicott's action, cooler heads hit upon the plan of substituting the royal arms for the offending cross in the canton of the flag. Later the arms were replaced by a distinctive local symbol, a pine tree. Such trees often served as village meeting places.

Another venture in heraldry sprang not from religious or democratic zeal but from cold-blooded commercialism. Early in the 1700's Colonial shipping had expanded to such an extent that it became advisable for merchant vessels to fly some sort of flag identifying them with a particular province. New York shippers, for example, adopted a white banner showing a black beaver (for the lucrative fur trade). And Massachusetts Bay ships flew a white emblem decorated with the now familiar New England pine tree. When independence was won these early Colonial banners became the ancestors of the modern state flags. (The pine tree still exists today on the reverse of the Massachusetts state flag.)

The widening gulf that developed between America and Great Britain after the French and Indian War was graphically illustrated in Colonial flags. At first the source of discontent sprang from what Americans re-

British Union (to 1776) (page 2)

British Red Ensign (to 1776) (page 3)

Spanish Flag (to 1785) (page 4)

French Flag (to 1789) (page 5)

garded as an infringement of inherent liberties. They dramatized their desires by posting mottoes on the British Red Ensign. At Taunton, Massachusetts, indignant townspeople gathered on the village green in 1774 and hoisted an ensign bearing the watchwords "Liberty and Union." (At this early date "union" probably referred to the Colonial desire for coequal status with England in a federation united by a common monarch, rather than to an effective organization of the thirteen provinces, still very much disunited.)

About the same time Pennsylvania patriots belonging to a local defense organization called the Associators raised a more decorative red ensign. It bore a coiled rattlesnake and the warning "Don't Tread on Me." This was the flag of John Proctor's Independent Battalion of Westmoreland County, Pennsylvania, as attested by the initials J.P. and I.B.W.C.P. lettered above the snake.

As the relationship between Colonies and mother country steadily worsened, patriot resentment became so strong that it could no longer be expressed by mottoes pasted or sewn on British flags. New banners were devised all along the Atlantic seaboard reflecting in heraldry the political opposition that had flamed up from economic coercion (nonimportation of British goods) to armed violence (the burning of the *Gaspee* and the Boston Tea Party). The Associators of Hanover, Pennsylvania, exemplified this increased defiance by resolving "That in the event of Great Britain attempting to force unjust laws upon us by the strength of arms, our cause we leave to Heaven and our rifles." To symbolize their intent, they adopted a red flag charged with a rifleman at the ready and the unequivocal choice, "Liberty or Death."

Another new banner was hoisted at Charleston, where two regiments of militia began strengthening the harbor defenses. Here the troop commander, Colonel (later General) William Moultrie, devised a simple blue flag with a white crescent in the canton.[1] This flag is sometimes reproduced with the addition of the crisp legend "Liberty" across the lower edge.

In most cases, however, these first distinctively American flags bore either a rattlesnake or a pine tree. In Pennsylvania and the Southern Colonies the popular design was a rattlesnake, viewed not as a repulsive reptile but as a symbol of vigilance and deadly striking power. One of the earliest of these banners represented the minutemen of Culpeper County, Virginia, a hotbed of Colonial discontent. A coiled rattler occupied the center of a white field, while above and below were the unmistakable sentiments "Liberty or Death" and "Don't Tread on Me." Two other important rattlesnake emblems were the Gadsden flag and the first naval jack, both described in the following chapter.

In New England, the pine-tree device predominated, sponsored primarily by the Massachusetts Bay colony,

[1] This is the flag rescued by Sergeant William Jasper when the British bombardment of Fort Sullivan (later Moultrie), June 28, 1776, shot away the flagstaff. Exposing himself to heavy fire, the heroic sergeant retrieved the banner and hoisted it again on a sponge staff. In October, 1779, at Savannah, Jasper fell fatally wounded trying to advance the colors of the Second South Carolina Regiment.

where it had appeared on English ensigns and had been minted on local coinage for at least a hundred years.[2] The proud pine tree appeared on at least two different types of banners hoisted over Colonial redoubts during the Battle of Bunker Hill (really Breed's Hill). Replicas of both flags hang in the Naval Academy Museum at Annapolis.

One of these was simply an old British blue ensign (blue field with St. George's cross in the canton) to which the Colonists had added a pine tree in the first quarter of the cross. It has come down in history as the Bunker Hill Flag.

The other emblem was red with a large pine centered in a white canton, the so-called Continental Flag. It is the flag shown in John Trumbull's painting "The Battle of Bunker Hill" (more properly called "The Death of Warren"). In general, such pictures are not to be trusted for historical accuracy. Trumbull, for example, conceived of his paintings as memorials rather than as attempts to reconstruct actual scenes. In this case, however, he seems to have reproduced an actual flag or at least one very similar to an existing flag. (A colonel of militia, Trumbull did not take part in the battle itself but he did serve at the siege of Boston as adjutant of a Connecticut regiment.)

For some Massachusetts rebels the British flags had

[2] These "pine-tree shillings," minted of metal seized from Spanish vessels, were bootleg coins. This practice enraged Charles II until a clever friend of the Colonies (believed to be Sir Charles Temple) explained that the tree was really an "oak" made in honor of the great oak in which the King had once hidden to escape Cromwell's pursuers.

become so inimical that they devised completely new banners with a green tree as the centerpiece, usually on a white field. In one such emblem it was a Liberty Tree, representing a stately old elm in Boston's Hanover Square. Under this tree the Sons of Liberty, one of the most active of Colonial opposition groups, often met, and here they planned the Boston Tea Party. On other flags, either from intent or because of inexact manufacture, the tree sometimes resembled an oak, fir, spruce, or even a willow. More often, however, the green tree was supposed to be a pine and was so portrayed. It is unfortunate that the names of these enterprising flag designers remain unknown today.

When American resentment flared into armed rebellion in 1775, the Pine-Tree Flag played a conspicuous military role. In September of that year patriots launched two floating batteries on the Charles River as part of the siege operations conducted against the British troops in Boston. Flying bravely above the wooden gun casements, in defiance of Howe's cannon, was the Pine-Tree emblem. Other batteries placed in the Delaware River to help defend the city of Philadelphia flew the same flag.

On the seas the Pine-Tree emblem served as America's first naval ensign. In the autumn of 1775 General Washington fitted out six so-called cruisers, commanded by army captains and manned by soldiers—the *Lynch, Franklin, Lee, Harrison, Warren,* and *Washington.* While workmen readied the vessels for war Washington's military secretary (adjutant general), Colonel Joseph Reed, wrote from Cambridge: "Please to fix some particular color for a flag, and a signal, by which our vessels may know one another. What do you think of a flag with a white ground, a tree in the middle, the motto 'Appeal to Heaven'? This is the flag of our floating batteries."

Only one vessel of this pathetic little fleet won a major military victory. On November 29, 1775, the *Lee*, commanded by robust John Manley, forced the surrender of the British brig *Nancy* and captured a treasured cargo of muskets, shot, powder, and a thirteen-inch brass mortar later named "Congress." Manley thus became the first American sea captain to win a naval battle and the Pine-Tree banner became the first American ensign to preside over such a victory. A second cruiser, the *Washington,* fell victim to H.M.S. *Fowey* on December 7—a date indelibly marked in history for another crushing American naval defeat 166 years later. The colors of the *Washington* were taken to the British Admiralty Office and accurately described in the *London Chronicle* the following month.

On April 29, 1776, the General Court of Massachusetts decided that for its provincial navy "the Uniform of Officers be Green and White . . . and that the Colours be a white Flagg, with a green Pine Tree, and an Inscription, 'Appeal to Heaven.'" Much as did the Stars and Stripes of a later day, this flag (despite the clarity of the law) received many improvisations. In one popular form the appeal was changed to "God" and two new devices were added—a coiled rattlesnake and the warning "Don't Tread on Me."

There is less evidence that the pine-tree flags received

a comparable usage in land warfare. But it is almost certain that some Massachusetts regiments carried such banners throughout the early months of fighting and even perhaps until the final victory at Yorktown. With such a prominent display at a critical hour in history the Pine-Tree emblem might well have become the national flag of America. One handicap it could not overcome, however. Its symbolism had become too closely associated with one particular colony, Massachusetts—or at best, New England. If a national flag was to be accepted by all the Colonies it must have something for everyone, because local pride was strong and loyalties were primarily directed toward the individual provinces.

No one can say which flag first gave representation to all thirteen Colonies in its symbolism. One early American banner showed thirteen mailed hands grasping an endless chain; another portrayed a mailed fist holding thirteen arrows. In some of the rattlesnake flags the snake possessed thirteen rattles.

The first American flag to represent the Colonies by means of thirteen stripes is believed to be the Markoe flag of the Philadelphia Light Horse Troop (later called First Troop of Philadelphia City Cavalry). It was a yellow flag with an elaborate coat of arms in the center and thirteen alternate blue and silver stripes in the canton. This flag is believed to have been designed by Captain Abram Markoe, a Danish subject who formed and equipped the twenty-eight-man troop at his own expense in 1774. In June, 1775, the troop had the honor of escorting General Washington from Philadelphia to

New York on his way to Cambridge to take command of Colonial troops assembled there. Late in 1775 Markoe was forced to resign his commission when King Christian VII of Denmark forbade his subjects to fight against England. But the troop and its flag stayed in service and saw action at Trenton, Princeton, Brandywine, and Germantown. (The flag is now preserved in the troop's armory, in Philadelphia.)

Another method of representing all the Colonies in early Revolutionary flags was by means of thirteen stars. The first flag known to have presented this device was that of the United Train of Artillery, a militia battery of Providence, organized in April, 1775. Its flag featured in the center of the field a snake, fouled anchor, two cannon, and two mottoes on scrolls, all encircled by thirteen five-pointed blue stars. The source of the stars is uncertain, as is the flag's date of origin; it is believed, however, to have been in use by 1776. In February, 1776, the First Rhode Island Regiment introduced the earliest American flag displaying thirteen white stars in the canton (of blue). The rows of stars were arranged 3-2-3-2-3, forming the combined crosses of St. George and St. Andrew—a design that was soon to become the standard method of arranging the stars in the national flags flown by the United States naval vessels. (Both of these Rhode Island flags are still preserved in Providence—the first in the Historical Society Museum, the other in the Statehouse.)

These, then, were the chief banners that represented America while scattered patriots of thirteen separate provinces struggled against a rule they found oppressive. For the moment most of the patriots sought only a peaceful redress of grievances. Few of them were ready to echo the sentiments of Sam Adams at Lexington early in the morning of April 19, 1775. Fleeing the clutch of General Gage's soldiers, Adams was hurrying across the fields when he heard the first burst of gunfire in the town. Turning to John Hancock, his companion in flight, Adams exulted: "Oh, what a glorious morning is this."

★ ★ ★ ★ ★

★ ★ ★ ★ ★

CHAPTER 3

THE FIRST NATIONAL FLAG

The year 1775 was full of uncertainty, confusion, and brief but bitter clashes between American militiamen and British troops. In April armed Colonists routed British regulars at Concord and two months later they battled savagely on Charlestown peninsula to keep the King's troops penned up in Boston. On July 2 General Washington took command of the New England militia around Boston to conduct siege operations against Sir William Howe's forces within the city. Washington also began organizing the rag, tag, and bobtail of assembled militiamen into a full-fledged army "for the defense of American liberty." Belligerent as these steps were, the Colonists were not yet openly rebellious. As late as July 8 the Continental Congress addressed a petition to King George III and signed it "Your Majesty's faithful subjects"!

By year's end a semblance of military order had been achieved and on January 1, 1776, the formation of the Continental Army was proclaimed at Washington's headquarters in Cambridge, Massachusetts. On the occasion the commander in chief wrote: "We had hoisted the Union Flag in compliment to the United Colonies." The flagpole was a seventy-six-foot schooner mast erected atop Prospect Hill[1] in nearby Somerville (then part of Charlestown). What Washington called the "Union Flag" others referred to by a variety of names—Continental Flag, Congress Flag, Cambridge Flag, the Colours of the United Colonies, Great Union, First Navy Ensign, Grand Union. Probably the most popular title, and the one that has lasted down to the present time, was Grand Union.

Thus on the day of its birth the Continental Army—the army that was to win independence for the United States—had its first flag. The banner was not startlingly new. It was merely the Meteor Flag of England with six horizontal white stripes drawn across the red field. Its origin was as uncertain as the times—its designer unknown, its adoption unrecorded, its usage unofficial. It has been speculated that the Grand Union was devised by the Congressional Committee—Thomas Lynch, Sr. (of South Carolina), Benjamin Harrison (of Virginia), and Benjamin Franklin (of Pennsylvania)—that met with Washington at Cambridge in October, 1775, to discuss army problems. This is pure conjecture without the support of the slightest evidence.

[1] Today on this hill a tablet commemorates the first hoisting of the Grand Union Flag.

The raising of the Grand Union also bred confusion. The British in Boston mistook the Continental Colors on Prospect Hill for their own army flag. They believed that its hoisting indicated the Colonists were ready to submit to the King's latest proclamation of authority over all Colonial affairs.

But the true intent behind the Grand Union did not long escape the British, particularly on the seas. Late in 1775 the Continental Congress had ordered the outfitting of eight new armed vessels. The new fleet began assembling at Philadelphia under the command of Esek Hopkins, an aggressive and outspoken sea captain. When warm weather unlocked the frozen Delaware River, Commodore Hopkins sailed out into the Atlantic and in March, 1776, boldly raided New Providence in the Bahamas. This naval victory netted about a hundred cannon and extensive military stores desperately needed by the poorly equipped Colonial forces. (Assisting in the capture was the first combat contingent of the United States Marine Corps, authorized by the Continental Congress the previous November.)

Historians have often disagreed over what flags were flown by Hopkins' flagship, the *Alfred*. The preponderance of evidence indicates that three flags were used— the ensign of the fleet, the personal flag of the commanding officer, and a naval jack. The ensign was the Grand Union. Its display is well documented by contemporary witnesses. One British spy at Philadelphia reported that the flagship was flying "English colours, *but more striped*." Another witness described the flag as "the Union Flag with thirteen stripes in the field, emblematical of the Thirteen United Colonies." A third eyewitness account comes from Hopkins' executive officer, the fiery John Paul Jones. In a letter to Minister of Marine Robert Morris, Jones told with pride that "It was my fortune, as the senior of the first Lieutenants, to hoist myself the Flag of America the first time it was displayed." Only the Grand Union could have been so described at that time.

The use of Hopkins' personal standard was also confirmed by firsthand observation. A New Providence reporter, after writing of a flag "striped under the Union with thirteen stripes," told of a second banner bearing a "rattlesnake and the motto 'Don't Tread on Me.'" This, then, was the so-called Gadsden flag, the emblem of Colonel Christopher Gadsden, a delegate from South Carolina and one of the original members of the Marine Committee of the Continental Congress. In February, 1776, the energetic colonel returned to Charleston from Philadelphia and presented the Provincial Congress with "an elegant Standard such as is to be used by the Commander-in-Chief of the American Navy; being a yellow field with a lively representation of a Rattlesnake in the middle, in the attitude of going to strike, and these words 'Don't Tread on Me.'"

There is less evidence to identify the third flag used by Hopkins' fleet—the one flown at the bow. The most common belief is that this emblem bore a serpent stretched diagonally across a field of thirteen alternate red and white stripes. It has survived in history as the First Navy Jack.

The use of two rattlesnake emblems in Hopkins' command may account for a change in the flag of the commanding officer reputed to have been made by the time the ships returned to New London. Most of Hopkins' men, as well as the commander himself, were from New England. They were more familiar with pine-tree flags than with the rattlesnake emblem since the latter was more closely associated with Pennsylvania and the Southern Colonies. As a result Hopkins is believed to have authorized a combination of the two designs in his personal flag. This must have been the banner referred to by a contemporary English writer: "A strange flag has lately appeared in our seas, bearing a pine tree with the portraiture of a rattlesnake coiled up at its roots, with these daring words, 'Don't tread on me.' We learn that the vessels bearing this flag have a sort of commission from a society of people at Philadelphia calling themselves the continental Congress."

Many of the original Revolutionary colors continued to fly throughout the war on both land and sea. They added a bright touch to what was often drab, disheartening duty for soldier and sailor alike. None of these flags, however, enjoyed the widespread respect accorded the Grand Union. Why was this gay emblem— never officially approved or formally recognized—so enthusiastically received? Why was it adopted by both the Army and Navy in different parts of the country at almost the same time?

The answer seems to be that it was perfectly adapted to the needs of the moment. Although the spirit of insurrection had been in the air for years, many people remained reluctant to take the bold step of open rebellion. They were "still feeding on the dainty food of reconciliation," as Washington phrased it. Yet there was a growing pride in the name "America" and in the strengthening union of its thirteen colonies. The Grand Union provided just the proper symbolism to represent this ambivalent attitude. By taking the colors of Great Britain's flags and by using the union device in the canton it illustrated the continuing bond between Colonies and king. At the same time, the flag was distinctive, unique, and representative of the swelling desire for self-government. The Grand Union belonged to no special colony, province, or group. It was an emblem whose symbolism was so catholic as to earn the respect of all —the Loyalist and the Patriot, the soldier and the planter, the defiant and the fearful.

For the first time, then, the American Colonists had a flag with nationalistic overtones. It was soon to be hoisted from Massachusetts to Georgia, flying from forts and barracks ashore and from the masts of naval vessels at sea. Although it was never carried as a battle flag on land, it was intimately linked with the momentous political and military events of the period. It flew in Boston after the British evacuated that city in March, 1776, in New York when Washington occupied Manhattan Island and Brooklyn Heights in April, and in Philadelphia while the Continental Congress was debating independence. North Carolina even decorated its paper currency with a fine reproduction of the Grand Union.

On July 2, 1776, when the "Representatives of the United States of America" voted independence from

Great Britain, the Continental Congress became the *de facto* government of the new nation and the Grand Union became its proud emblem. But there was true irony in the situation. Even as the Declaration of Independence automatically promoted the Grand Union to the status of a national banner, it rendered the flag obsolete. The political ties with Great Britain were now snapped irrevocably and the crosses of St. Andrew and St. George in the canton of the Grand Union became an anachronism. They were also an infuriating reminder of oppressive British government—the Stamp Act, the Townshend duties on tea and other imports, the Boston Massacre, the Five Intolerable Acts, and now the insulting burden of military occupation. The crosses must go!

The incongruity of the Grand Union's symbolism failed to impress Congress immediately. That body was justly occupied with "our Lives, our Fortunes and our Sacred Honor" and could not take up promptly the question of a substitute banner. It was almost a full year later (on June 14, 1777) that the first flag legislation was enacted. Meanwhile the Grand Union continued to serve both on land and at sea. On July 9, 1776, at the Battery on Manhattan Island, Washington ordered that his troops be read the Declaration of Independence "with an audible voice." After the reading the Grand Union was hoisted over the commander's headquarters. Admiral Lord Howe's confidential secretary, Ambrose Searle, reported the incident: "They have set up their standard in the fort upon the southern point of the town. Their colours are thirteen stripes of red and white alternately, with the union canton in the corner." Poor heraldic terminology but accurate reporting!

The Grand Union also flew from the mainmast of the schooner *Royal Savage*, the flagship of Benedict Arnold's makeshift fleet assembled on Lake Champlain. (Arnold himself fought aboard the *Congress*, a galley.) And it presumably went down with the ship when Arnold lost every vessel during the one-sided battle of Valcour Island, October 11–12.

A happier event occurred the following month when the Grand Union received the first foreign salute accorded an American flag. This was an eleven-gun volley fired by a Dutch West Indies fort (Fort Orange), acknowledging a similar salute given by the *Andrew Doria* (named for the Genoese admiral Andrea Doria), one of the vessels in Hopkins' original fleet. Later the Dutch governor of St. Eustatius Island was recalled when the British sharply protested this salute to a "brigantine" flying "the flag of His Majesty's rebellious subjects."

The Grand Union probably followed the Continental Congress from Philadelphia to Baltimore that December when British troops threatened the capital from New Jersey. And it must have returned to Philadelphia with the Congress two months later after the Continental Army had lashed back at Trenton and Princeton. If Washington carried any flag across the Delaware River Christmas night, 1776, he carried the Grand Union and not the Stars and Stripes as shown in Emanuel Leutze's painting "Washington Crossing the Delaware." No

Dutch India Company Flag (page 6)

New Sweden Flag (page 7)

Proctor's Independent Battalion (page 13)

Hanover Associators (page 13)

William Moultrie (page 14)

Culpeper County, Virginia (page 14)

Bunker Hill (page 15)

First Naval Ensign (page 16)

stars and stripes banner had yet been designed or approved. (And, just as surely, Leutze erred in picturing the American commander in chief. Washington was too good a soldier to stand up in an open boat navigating a swift river clogged with floating ice.) It is also likely that the Grand Union floated over the headquarters of the Continental Army at Morristown, New Jersey, that winter.

When the Grand Union was finally supplanted by the Stars and Stripes its passing was as shadowy as its origin. No records show when it was last used at sea. On land, it is known to have been hoisted as late as August 3, 1777, during the British siege of Fort Schuyler (formerly Fort Stanwix) in New York State. Some historians have erroneously claimed that the Stars and Stripes was first hoisted at this date and place. But this claim ignores the incontestable fact that although the flag legislation was passed in June, the act was not officially published until four full weeks after General St. Leger had laid siege to the patriot garrison on the Mohawk. It also neglects the irrefutable testimony of the besieged. Colonel Marinus Willett, second in command to Colonel Peter Gansevoort at Fort Schuyler, provided a detailed narrative of the action. He reported that on the night of August 2–3 the patriots improvised a "Continental Flag" by using red and white "stripes" and blue "strips" cut from garments donated by members of the garrison. *Strips* would be a strange way indeed to fashion the square blue canton of the Stars and Stripes! Undoubtedly the strips were the eight blue triangles of the British Union in the canton. And there is no mention at all of stars. (The blue strips came from the cloak of thrifty Captain Abraham Swartwout, who presented a bill for the destroyed garment a year later.)

Another defender of the fort, Lieutenant William Colbrath, wrote in his journal: "Early this morning [August 3, 1777] a Continental flag, made by the officers of Colonel Gansevoort's regiment, was hoisted and a cannon leveled at the enemy's camp was fired on the occasion." Corroborating evidence that the Fort Schuyler flag was the Grand Union comes from a carving on a powder horn owned by John McGraw, one of the fort's soldiers in the autumn of 1777. With loving care McGraw carved out a reproduction of the fort showing a flag hoisted above it—the Grand Union—and when finished he inscribed the date "December 25, 1777." This date will live longer in history as Christmas Day at Valley Forge.

CHAPTER 4

★ ★ ★ ★ ★

★ ★ ★ ★ ★

BIRTH OF A NEW ▨

CONSTELLATION ▨

Following Washington's victories at Trenton and Princeton the Continental Congress returned to Philadelphia in the spring of 1777. The situation remained grim at best. Sir William Howe's forces occupied New York City less than a hundred miles away. Between the legislators and the enemy army were General Washington's Continentals, as usual poorly equipped and badly outnumbered. While both sides maneuvered for advantage in New Jersey the Congress continued to meet in the Statehouse (now called Independence Hall), discharging all the duties that fall upon a single operating branch of government.

Much of the Congress' work consisted of a wearying attentiveness to minor detail and petty routine. It was with the aim of disposing of just such small matters that the members assembled June 14, 1777. A large share of the business transacted that day was taken care of by simple resolutions not requiring discussion or debate. For example one resolution appropriated various sums to three Army captains "for the use of their respective independent companies." Another took steps to aid New Yorkers "immediately distressed for want of salt."

Several resolutions stemmed from recommendations of the Marine Committee:

> RESOLVED, That the Marine Committee be impowered to give such directions respecting the Continental ships of war in the river Delaware as they think proper in case the enemy succeed in their attempts on said river.
>
> The Council of the State of Massachusetts Bay having represented by letter to the president of Congress that Captain John Roach, some time since appointed to command the Continental ship of war *Ranger,* is a person of doubtful character and ought not to be entrusted with such a command; therefore
>
> RESOLVED, That Captain John Roach be suspended until the Navy Board for the eastern department shall have enquired fully into his character and report thereon to the Marine Committee.[1]
>
> RESOLVED, That Captain John Paul Jones be appointed to command the said ship *Ranger.*

Sandwiched among these transient decisions was one of lasting significance:

> RESOLVED, That the flag of the thirteen United States be thirteen stripes, alternate red and white; that

[1] Either Massachusetts or the Congress was badly confused here. John Roach had never been appointed to such a command and was in fact not even an officer in the Continental Navy!

the union be thirteen stars, white in a blue field, representing a new constellation.

At last the new United States had a national flag, officially designed and formally adopted. And it was a flag that all the people could take to their hearts, for each state was doubly represented—by a stripe and a star— and the union of the states was doubly signified—in the field and in the canton.

This simple, direct resolution was the beginning, the middle, and the end of Congressional information concerning the original flag law. It is unfortunate that the Congress chose to be so terse in passing this legislation. A vote of thanks to the designer, an appropriation for services rendered, or even an indirect reference to some individual would have spotlighted the origin of the flag and left no doubt in the minds of future generations. But such was not the case and today the first flag law stands stark and isolated among the annals of the time. Among other contemporary records—official, semi-official, and private—there is nothing to reveal or even hint at what provided the basis of the resolution.

This lack of documentation has produced an interesting development, unforeseen in 1777 and for that matter unforeseen during the lifetime of the Revolutionary fathers. In later years historical speculators have seized upon the absence of records and clear-cut evidence to construct their own theories of origin before June 14, 1777. As a result, today there exists a whole series of stories, each revealing the "true" beginning of the Stars and Stripes. The pattern of construction is much the same in each—an actual Revolutionary figure, one or several indisputable points of historical reference, and then a quick conclusion based upon inferences and deductions that often recklessly misuse established data. Most of these stories grew out of strong ancestral devotion or a superabundance of local pride. Seldom have the creating motives been for selfish reasons or commercial gain.

The most prominent theories of flag origin are those built around Betsy Ross, John Hulbert, George Washington, Francis Hopkinson, the town of Easton, Pennsylvania, John Paul Jones, Abram Markoe, and the Rhode Island colonial flags. These theories are of course mutually contradictory. In general they are also overly romantic, incapable of proof, and unconvincing in one or more vital points.

★ ★ ★ ★ ★ THE MAKING OF A LEGEND

By far the best-known claim for the origin of the Stars and Stripes is the Betsy Ross story. This account strikes such a warm and appealing note that it has survived through the years despite the seemingly mortal blows repeatedly dealt it by distinguished researchers, scholars, and historians.

The Betsy Ross story relates that in May or June of 1776 George Washington, Robert Morris, and George Ross were appointed to a committee charged with designing a national flag. Washington is reputed to have prepared a design which was then taken to the Philadelphia home of Elizabeth Ross, widow of committeeman Ross's nephew, John. Mrs. Ross, an expert seamstress, made a flag from this sketch, changing only the number of points on each star from six to five. The stars themselves are said to have been placed in a circle in the blue canton. (One version goes back to King Arthur's Round Table as a source for this arrangement!) The story concludes abruptly with Washington personally showing the flag to the "grateful" Congress.

Now it is true that the commander in chief did spend May 23 to June 5 in Philadelphia. He had been summoned to the city by the Congress for urgent conferences on the operations of the Army. The grave military weaknesses of the Colonies plus the growing agitation for independence left Washington little time to meditate or work on such secondary problems as the creation of a national ensign. Nor do the detailed *Journals* of the Continental Congress even hint at the formation of a flag committee or a report from such a group—and the reporting member was supposedly George Washington, the most respected military figure on the continent, whose every word and action received the closest attention.

The Betsy Ross story first came to light in 1870 in a paper read by her grandson, Willam J. Canby, before the Historical Society of Pennsylvania. This paper was based on conversations Canby said he had with his maternal grandmother prior to her death in 1836, when he was eleven years old and Mrs. Ross eighty-four. According to Canby, his recollections of the conversations, plus supplementary information from his mother's generation, were written down in 1857 and published thirteen years later—a total of ninety-four years after the related flag-making event took place. To support his claim, Canby secured affidavits from several local residents, all interested parties, well advanced in age, who were likewise relying upon memory and hearsay to recall something in the distant past. In point of time, the affidavits were secured *after* the Canby paper was prepared.

Canby's story quickly gained circulation in contemporary newspapers, magazines, and books. As it spread, other bits of "evidence" accumulated. In 1879 a Boston paper published an alleged picture of Betsy Ross which was widely copied. It was pure artistic license for no pictures or other likenesses were ever made of the seamstress. Eight years later the "flag house" itself was "located" at 239 Arch Street, Philadelphia, although there was no real proof Mrs. Ross ever lived there and much valid evidence that she did not. Later the residence was variously fixed at numbers 233, 235, and 241, all on Arch Street. By now, however, the Canby-Ross tale had been repeated so often and had acquired so many roots that it defied challenge even in part. This despite the repeated discrediting of supporting evidence as contradictory, confused, and uncorroborated.

The grand total of provable facts in the Betsy Ross legend are: (1) that Betsy Ross was a patriot needle-woman of Philadelphia, twice widowed by the Revolutionary War; (2) that she made some Pennsylvania naval flags, receiving from the state Naval Board on May 29, 1777, fourteen pounds, twelve shillings, two pence. (It has never been ascertained what these flags looked like.) Of such flimsy material are constructed the cherished legends of American history.

★ ★ ★ ★ ★   A GENESIS ON LONG ISLAND?

Of all the claims made for the origin of the Stars and Stripes, one account places the flag far earlier in time than any of the others. This is the claim for the Hulbert, or Bridgehampton, flag supposedly made in 1775—a year before Washington's alleged chat with Betsy Ross in Philadelphia and two years before the first flag law of June 14, 1777. Most of the interest in the Hulbert flag has been generated on Long Island, a place rich in historical associations and almost as rich in historians.

The story of the Hulbert flag claim begins in July, 1775, when John Hulbert, a cordwainer and magistrate, became captain of a company of Long Island minutemen. Two months later Hulbert's company moved to Ticonderoga to assist in the campaign to liberate the Champlain Valley. In November the Long Islanders escorted a group of British prisoners back to Trenton and Hulbert reported to the Continental Congress in Philadelphia. After a short tour of duty at Fort Constitution (Lee) on the Hudson, the company returned to their homes for discharge January 18, 1776. Hulbert resumed his residence in Suffolk County and turned to privateering.

Exactly a hundred and fifty years later, in 1926, a tattered old flag was found in a house once occupied by John Hulbert. The location of the house is uncertain. One report says it was in Bridgehampton; another says Sag Harbor. This banner—which looks almost too much as an original model should look—was soon heralded as the prototype of the Stars and Stripes. One version of the story relates that the flag was made on Long Island before Hulbert's company left for Ticonderoga; another version says that it was made in the Champlain Valley to rival the banner of the British Seventh (Royal Fusiliers) Regiment of Foot, captured at Fort Chambly, October 18, 1775. (This color contained the conventional St. George and St. Andrew crosses.)

Regardless of its place of origin, the heart of the Hulbert flag claim lies in what is supposed to have taken place in Philadelphia when Hulbert reported to the Congress in November. Proponents of this account say that he brought the flag with him and that Francis Hopkinson, a delegate from New Jersey, may have been asked to make a sketch of it. This sketch supposedly formed the basis of the later flag resolution. All this is highly speculative and greatly weakened by the fact that Hopkinson did not arrive in Philadelphia to take his seat in the Congress until seven months later, on June 28, 1776. At this point, though, the Hulbert account falls silent, leaving a large, unexplained void of nineteen months in the evolution of the national flag.

There can be little doubt that the Hulbert flag is of the Revolutionary era. Its workmanship and its thirteen six-pointed stars confirm this. There is little reason to believe, however, that it predates the first flag resolution of 1777. A more likely explanation is that Hulbert did not acquire the flag until the Stars and Stripes had become generally familiar. During all the time he kept a journal, 1770 to 1805, he failed to mention the flag, and when he moved to western New York in 1807 he left the banner behind.

The design of the Hulbert flag is also unlikely for

42 ★ *Flags of the U.S.A.*

1775. Its representation of the thirteen Colonies in both stars and stripes signifies a cohesive union among the colonies that was not a fact for many months. Moreover, it anticipates in heraldry a complete break with the mother country. At this time devotion to England was still strong and American efforts were directed chiefly toward reconciliation, not independence, in flag or in fact. The adoption and popular acceptance of the British crosses in the Grand Union Flag of even later date illustrates more accurately the prevailing mood of the Continentals.

★ ★ ★ ★ ★   THE SOURCE AT SULGRAVE
MANOR?
One school of supertraditionalists traces the lineage of the Stars and Stripes back to Sulgrave Manor in sixteenth-century England. This apparently provides the flag with the necessary *correct* background and genealogy.

As with the other legends of origin, the historical references in this story are impeccable. Lawrence Washington, early ancestor of George, became grantee and lord of Sulgrave Manor in 1539. The coat of arms acquired by this first Lord of Sulgrave was of course retained in the Washington family when they migrated to Virginia and so was later inherited by the commander in chief. The arms consisted of a silver shield emblazoned with two red bars and three red mullets, or molets (heraldic stars with five points), crested with a raven. End of fact, beginning of fiction.

Early in the nineteenth century it was suggested in England that the American flag was copied from the Washington arms. This unfounded assumption went unnoticed until the time of the Philadelphia Centennial Exposition of 1876. Then Martin Farquhar Tupper, a popular English romancer, wrote his drama *Washington*, aimed at cultivating good feeling between Great Britain and America. In this work Tupper speaks for Benjamin Franklin:

> ". . . I proposed it to the Congress.
> It was the leader's old Crusading blazon.
> Washington's coat, his own heraldic shield.
> And on the spur, when we must choose a flag
> Symboling independent unity,
> We, and not he—all was unknown to him—
> Took up his coat of arms and multiplied
> And magnified it in every way, to this
> Our glorious national banner."

It made little difference that on June 14, 1777, Franklin was not a member of the Congress or even in America but in France. Tupper's dream was widely accepted and another legend was born.

The connection between the design of the Washington arms and the national ensign is considerably removed. There is no hint of blue color (azure) anywhere in the arms. The heraldic "stars" are red, emblazoned on a silver background and pierced with a central hole. And the adoption of the mullet device would hardly constitute a "new constellation" as specifically prescribed by the flag resolution.

The presumed acceptance of the design by the Congress is equally farfetched. Can it be believed that at the height of Revolutionary strife the legislators would be interested in securing an English ancestry for their national flag—and one of nobility at that? It is also impossible to conceive of the modest Washington permitting any such personal exploitation. In answer to a query about his family escutcheon he once wrote: "This is a subject to which I confess I have paid very little attention." Even assuming these obstacles could have been overcome (and who could have been pushing the project?), what of Washington's more vitriolic critics, particularly those who supposedly feared that he was intent upon dictatorship or monarchy? The promotion of his arms at that time would certainly have exploded a reaction echoing down to present times. Yet no word of comment or reproach on this score was ever advanced during the general's lifetime or later.

In heraldic terms the Washington arms are: argent, two bars and in chief three molets (mullets) gules. Similarly, the original flag would have been described as: gules, six barrulets argent, a canton azure charged with thirteen molets argent. The rebelling Americans had forcibly demonstrated that they were through with royalty. It was now palpably clear that they were also done with heraldry.

Despite the absence of supporting proof this theory of origin has been repeated again and again in various publications. One recent source is an English book on heraldry published during the 1950's. The proponents of this theory evidently remain unsatisfied that the Washington arms do live in one "gules and argent" American flag, that of the District of Columbia, adopted in 1938.

DESIGNING

Of all the "legitimate" claims made for originating the Stars and Stripes only one was publicly stated contemporaneously with the adoption of the flag. The claimant was Francis Hopkinson of New Jersey, one of the signers of the Declaration of Independence. Hopkinson's claim is also unique in that it was advanced by the man himself—not by a devoted descendent, a romantic versifier, or a sentimental antiquarian.

Hopkinson was a man of demonstrated literary ability[2] and a student of heraldry. Elected to the Continental Congress June 22, 1776, he resigned in November to serve as chairman of a three-man Navy Board, the executive arm of the Congress' Marine Committee at Philadelphia. He later served as Treasurer of Loans for the United States and as judge of admiralty for the state of Pennsylvania. In 1780 Hopkinson publicized his self-confessed contribution to the flag in a letter to the Board of Admiralty, the first successor to the Marine Committee.

After expressing pleasure at the Admiralty Board's approval of the device he had submitted for its official seal Hopkinson wrote:

I have with great readiness upon several occasions exerted my small abilities in this way for the public service,

[2] His best-known work was a humorous ballad "The Battle of the Kegs," which described an incident on the Delaware River during the British occupation of Philadelphia.

as I flatter myself, to the satisfaction of those I wish to please, viz:

The Flag of the United States of America.
Seven devices for the Continental Currency.
A Seal for the Board of Treasury . . .
A Great Seal for the United States of America, with a Reverse.

For these services he asked for "a quarter cask of the public wine" as "proper and reasonable reward for these labours of fancy and a suitable encouragement to others of the like nature."

Had Hopkinson's request been granted it would have established beyond doubt the identity of the flag designer. But no payment in "public wine" or anything else was made. A more formal bill was then presented to the Congress asking payment for the design of "the great Naval Flag of the United States" and numerous other items. (The national flag and the naval ensign, or "great Naval Flag," have always been one and the same.) This time the total charges were not expressed in terms of thirst but in "hard money," amounting to $7200 (£2700) Continental money, at sixty for one.

For four months the bill was bucked back and forth within the Treasury Department. Finally, on October 27, 1780, payment was refused. It was explained that Hopkinson could not claim authorship because he "was not the only person consulted on those exhibitions of Fancy." The Congress confirmed this judgment on August 23, 1781, when it resolved "That the report relative to the fancy-work of F. Hopkinson ought not be acted on."

Embittered, Hopkinson resigned as Treasurer of Loans and abandoned attempts to collect for his heraldic labors. His on-the-spot requests for payment indicate that he was somehow connected with the preparation of a design for the national flag. But the verdicts of the Treasury Department and the Congress leave little room to believe that he was entitled to a claim of sole designership.

Hopkinson's 1780 bill for designing the Great Seal is also highly suspect. The seal was not adopted by the Congress until June 20, 1782. Credit for its design is usually given to William Barton, a private citizen of Philadelphia, and Charles Thomson, secretary of the Congress.

★ ★ ★ ★ ★ A STRIPES AND STARS AT EASTON

For well over one hundred years a colorful red, white, and blue flag has hung in the public library at Easton, Pennsylvania. The banner has often earned a quick double-take from unwary visitors because of its curious design. It contains all the devices of the national flag but in reversed position—the thirteen red and white stripes occupy the canton while the white stars stand out on a fly of blue.

Throughout the nineteenth century this flag was honored as the company color carried by Captain Abraham Horn's Northampton County men in the last year of the War of 1812. Then about 1900 there began an ambitious project to promote this banner into "the first Stars and Stripes of the United Colonies." Its history

Philadelphia Light Horse Troop (page 18)

Providence Artillery (page 19)

First Rhode Island Regiment (page 19)

Grand Union (page 22)

First Navy Jack (page 24)

Gadsden Flag (page 24)

So-Called Betsy Ross Flag (page 38)

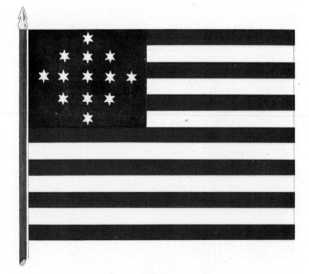

Hulbert Flag (page 41)

was rewritten so that it became the actual flag unfurled at Easton on July 8, 1776, the date on which news of independence first reached Northampton County. As such, of course, it easily could have been the source for the national flag adopted by Congress the following year. It could have been, but it undoubtedly was not.

The chief arguments for ascribing a Revolutionary origin to the Easton flag consist of the usual speculations and inferences. The only points of evidence are two newspaper references to a standard raised at Easton courthouse during the first reading of the Declaration of Independence there on July 8. There is no description of the flag except that it contained an unidentified symbol or inscription relating to the thirteen Colonies. The display of such a device can scarcely be called evidence that this banner was the Easton flag of later date. By mid-1776 many flags illustrated some form of union. Chief of these, of course, was the Grand Union, then at the height of its popularity. The thirteen broad stripes of this familiar flag are a much more likely vehicle for the symbolism reported in the newspapers than a flag of uncertain origin.

After the courthouse flag raising, this shadowy emblem passes into oblivion. Then thirty-eight years later it miraculously reappears in a presentation to Captain Horn's company. And here is where the Easton claim falls of its own weight. Contemporary witnesses report that in August, 1814, the flag was made by local ladies during a four-day period when Horn's and one other company were being outfitted for Army duty. Contemporary and near-contemporary historians make no mention of any earlier historical significance attached to the banner. When the flag was formally deposited in the library in 1821 there was no hint that it had any history other than its use in 1814. In fact there was not even a tradition of Colonial usage until as late as 1895! Then for the first time the question of possible eighteenth-century origin was raised. By 1908 the unanswered question had ballooned into the first published claim (*Easton Daily Free Press,* February 25) that the surviving flag was the striped and starred banner of 1776. And another legend was born.

Those who accept the Easton priority claim point out that if the flag had not been made until 1814 it should have had fifteen stars and fifteen stripes arranged in the conventional manner. What this argument overlooks however is that the flag was made to be a company color and therefore some kind of distinctive design was in order. A regulation national flag could not have been used by ground troops at that time. No Army unit was authorized to carry the Stars and Stripes into battle until the Mexican War.

★ ★ ★ ★ ★   AS MANY THEORIES AS STRIPES

As a supplement to the major legends purporting to reveal the origin of the Stars and Stripes there is another whole series of minor myths. One of these relates that the tricolored, three-striped Netherlands flag contributed the design of the American ensign. While the United States did borrow money from the Netherlands there is nothing to indicate that it borrowed also from the Dutch flag. Similarly lacking in proof is the theory that members of Congress asked John Paul Jones to advise them on the design of a national ensign. This bold and efficient sea captain had many talents but heraldry was not numbered among them. A related story is that the flag was adopted by the Congress chiefly for the protection of Jones, a Scot, who might have been charged with treason if he had been captured under an emblem other than an "official" national banner. Such stories do credit to their authors' imaginations but not to their sense of history.

There has also been speculation that the Markoe flag supplied the inspiration for the thirteen stripes incorporated into the national ensign. This theory necessarily assumes that the blue and silver stripes in its canton were the direct ancestor of the red and white stripes in the field of the Grand Union, a line of descent unsupported by fact or strong tradition. A similar lack of continuity exists between the stars of the Rhode Island flags and the "new constellation" described by the Congress.

What, then, was the origin of the Stars and Stripes? The simple truth is that no one knows. Nor can anyone with reasonable certainty identify the designer or maker of the first starred and striped banner. No individual or group ever received contemporary recognition for such a project. And despite the most intensive research by capable historians the true story of the flag's birth remains unknown today.

This complete absence of evidence suggests that the flag had no single ancestor nor any one designer. It was simply the logical culmination of Revolutionary heraldry. The pattern, colors, and proportions had already been established by the Grand Union. The symbolism of the thirteen stripes was as appropriate for the states as it had been for the Colonies. Even the blue ground of the canton could not be improved. It provided a pleasing contrast to the red and white in the field. Only the noxious crosses had to be discarded and a felicitous charge found for the canton.

It is unlikely that the Marine Committee first studied all the banners then on display. Had they done so the association of stars with Rhode Island might well have ruled out that device. It was imperative that no local symbol be adopted. The rigors of war were already creating some ill feeling among the states, particularly between those of New England and the rest of the nation. Therefore a device with wide popular appeal had to be found. What could have been more natural—and pleasing—than to break up the blue ground with white stars? And thirteen of them, of course, one to represent each state. The opportunity to give double significance to the union was too good to be overlooked.

Any other choice would surely have evoked comment in the Congress. The legislators—and the people—were tense and worried, quick to accuse or to take offense. On the same day the flag was adopted the Congress officially reprimanded Gunning Bedford of Delaware. He was called before "the bar" to "ask pardon of the House and of the member challenged," Jonathan Sergeant, a delegate from New Jersey. Yet the adoption of a national flag, always a disputatious subject and a matter of great interest, provoked no formal discussion whatsoever. Outside Congress there was also a significant lack of comment. Although the appearance of the Grand Union produced widespread mention, the Stars and Stripes came into use almost unnoticed. It may be assumed then that the people as well as the Congress regarded the new flag as a natural descendant of the Grand Union, the substitution of stars for crosses a small, logical change.

Exactly how the Marine Committee arrived at its flag report is unknown, and probably unknowable, today. It was, however, the natural agency to spearhead the adoption of a national ensign. Navies have always taken the lead in flag matters. At sea a flag has long been a quick and positive means of identification. A ship without a national ensign is liable to a charge of piracy. Moreover, the infant United States Navy was probably more continental in organization and viewpoint than any other arm of the government, and thus more conscious of a need for a national banner.

What was this Marine Committee whose report resulted in the Congressional resolution adopting the Stars and Stripes? It was an executive body created by the Congress on December 11, 1775, to handle the naval affairs of the Colonies. Three days after its formation one member from each province was appointed to serve on the committee. It functioned until December, 1779, when it was replaced by a five-man Board of Admiralty.

One of the committee's big problems was to get enough members together to transact necessary business. Rarely did a majority of its membership attend committee meetings. Finally, on June 6, 1777, the Congress authorized a legal quorum of five members. The committee also suffered from frequent changes in personnel, in part unavoidable because of changes in the membership of the Congress itself. The existing records of the committee are so fragmentary that it is impossible to determine the members of the committee in attendance when the report on the flag was formulated. The number might have varied from the necessary quorum of five up to thirteen.

According to the *Journals* of the Congress the members of the committee on June 14, 1777, were: Nathan Browson (Georgia); Thomas Burke (North Carolina); Abraham Clark (New Jersey); John Hancock (Massachusetts), who served as president of the committee as well as president of the Congress; Richard Henry Lee (Virginia); Philip Livingston (New York); Henry Marchant (Rhode Island); Arthur Middleton (South Carolina); Robert Morris (Pennsylvania); Roger Sherman (Connecticut); William Smith (Maryland); Nicholas Van Dyke (Delaware); and William Whipple (New Hampshire).

From these men, then, came the impetus that led to the adoption of the first official flag of the United States. Their contribution lacked the charm and glamour that so many writers have insisted must be a part of the flag's origin. These men were simply practical legislators and executives, intent upon nothing more romantic than waging a war for the independence of a newborn nation.

CHAPTER 5

★ ★ ★ ★ ★

★ ★ ★ ★ ★

FLAG AND FREEDOM

SECURED

The tangled web of legends seeking to establish the origin of the national flag is rivaled in American history only by the great variety of claims made for the first public hoisting of the Stars and Stripes and its first display in ground combat. There are at least a score of such claims, most of them staked out with an excess of patriotic zeal and a shortage of substantiating evidence.

Any claim that the Stars and Stripes was raised prior to June 14, 1777, is without factual foundation. No such flag has been found to exist before the passage of the Congressional resolution. The claims made for a "first" display immediately after that date are equally lacking in proof. These stories are backstopped only by so-called logic and ingenious inference. For example, it is more than improbable that this banner was hoisted over

Washington's headquarters at Middlebrook, New Jersey, the following day, or that it flew anywhere on the first anniversary of the Declaration of Independence. Of a similar nature are the reports that the Stars and Stripes flew at Hubbardton, Vermont, on July 7 and at Fort Anne, New York, on July 9.

Later "first" claims must receive more careful consideration if only because of the possibility that the flag in question *might* have been based on the Congressional act of June 14. Although the official promulgation of the resolution was not made until September 3, at Philadelphia, it is certain that unofficial sources revealed the existence of the flag law before that time. The earliest known mention of the law was made in a diary kept by Ezra Stiles, clergyman friend of Franklin and later president of Yale University. Under date of July 9, 1777, Stiles wrote: "The Congress have substituted a new Constellation of 13 Stars (instead of the Union) in the Continental Colors."

The first known report of the resolution's full text was not made until August 3. This information was recorded in a journal kept by Dr. James Thacher, an Army surgeon then stationed at Albany. On that date Thacher wrote: "It appears by the papers that Congress resolved on the 14th of June last, that the flag of the thirteen United States be thirteen stripes, alternate red and white; that the Union be thirteen stars, white on a blue field."[1] Thus it is clear that by late July or early August knowledge of the new flag was beginning to spread through the new nation.

[1] The first public newspaper to carry the text of the resolution was the *Pennsylvania Evening Post,* under date of August 30.

These first unofficial reports have often been exploited to shore up the hardiest legend regarding the flag's first appearance in battle—the Fort Schuyler story discussed in chapter 3. Much of the blame for the persistence of this groundless claim rests on what was formerly called the War Department. In 1926 the department announced that "the Stars and Stripes got its baptism of fire in a land battle in the defense of Fort Stanwix, N.Y., on August 2, 1777." (Fort Stanwix, built in 1758 as a frontier post against the French, had fallen into ruin long before the Revolutionary War. In 1776 a new fort was erected on the site and named in honor of the often maligned New York patriot General Philip Schuyler.)

This "official" finding for Fort Schuyler brought sharp protests from careful students of flag history. The embarrassed War Department hastily withdrew its statement, reconsidered, and then announced in May, 1927, that the Fort Schuyler flag was not the Stars and Stripes. Two months later the original statement was again released to the press! A second time the Department retreated in confusion and published a correction. The retraction was complete and unqualified but, as usual, it received less publicity than the original declaration and the roots of the Fort Schuyler legend remained deeply implanted.

It is unfortunate that the War Department's final judgment on the Fort Schuyler controversy did not give proper credit to the actual flag flown by the besieged garrison. Acting Secretary of War B. H. Wells stated only that "while it bore stripes [it] bore no stars." Additional research would have established that the flag in question was none other than the long-neglected Grand Union.

The siege of Fort Schuyler in 1777 marked a turning point in the heretofore successful British drive on Albany. By blocking off the important Mohawk Valley the Fort Schuyler troops prevented Colonel St. Leger from effecting a junction with Burgoyne at the Hudson River. Burgoyne then turned to his left flank and sent the German commander Baum toward Bennington, Vermont, a vital supply base for New England and New York troops. American forces under General John Stark and Colonel Seth Warner marched out from Bennington to meet Baum. Stark exhorted his men: "Tonight the American flag floats over yonder hill or Molly Stark sleeps a widow." By sundown on August 16 the encircled Hessian force had surrendered, Baum lay dying on the battlefield, and Molly Stark was preparing to welcome her husband home. This victory paralyzed Burgoyne's invasion force and made possible the decisive triumph at Saratoga two months later.

The Battle of Bennington is believed to mark the first appearance of an American flag bearing thirteen stars and thirteen stripes. Although this claim is not backed up by direct comtemporary evidence it is supported by three strong arguments: (1) the flag associated with the battle is still preserved in the Bennington Historical Museum and remains unchallenged as the oldest Stars and Stripes in existence;[2] (2) the claim is corroborated

[2] The oldest flag to have thirteen white stars on a blue canton is also owned by the Bennington Historical Museum. Although little more than the canton remains, the flag is presumed to have had a green field. As such it was carried by Green Mountain

by a coherent and continuous local tradition that dates back to the day of the battle; and (3) it is generally accepted by almost every historian and scholar who has investigated and reported on Burgoyne's campaign and the Revolutionary history of the New Hampshire Grants, as Vermont was then called.

The Bennington battle flag was originally owned by Nathaniel Fillmore, grandfather of Millard Fillmore, the thirteenth President of the United States. Nathaniel Fillmore was a lieutenant in Captain Elijah Dewey's militia company that fought at Bennington. The flag remained in the Fillmore family for more than a century and then was returned to Bennington in 1926 as its most suitable home.

Of all the claims made for the "first" Stars and Stripes, this flag has the clearest record and the most historical merit. Despite its unusual design it is impossible to believe that this banner had any source other than the flag resolution of June 14. Doctor Thacher's journal has revealed that unofficial news of the resolution had reached the Northern Army at least as early as August 3. The flag designer may have misunderstood the actual wording of the "thirteen alternate red and white stripes," or he may have deliberately arranged them white and red in accordance with the principles of heraldry. The use of the figure 76 can only be explained as a method of honoring in blazonry the year of independence. The arrangement of the stars and the number of points in each were of course left to the imagination

troops at Bennington and later preserved by descendants of General Stark.

of each designer until specified by statute 135 years later.

The extent of the claims made for the Bennington Flag ends with its early display, however. It represented only a private interpretation of the flag law. There is no proof that it was an "official" flag of the United States Army or government.

Two months after the battle of Bennington the first Stars and Stripes is supposed to have presided over Burgoyne's surrender at Saratoga. Accounts of its display vary considerably. One is that such a flag flew over the tent of the commander in chief, General Horatio Gates. Another version relates that it was carried at the head of a parade of victorious American troops. Also present is the familiar story of how the flag was made by patriot women cutting up their flannel petticoats in a burst of patriotic devotion. No Revolutionary flag story would be complete without this charming bit of make-believe.

Despite the continuing tradition that the Stars and Stripes was raised at Saratoga there is not a shred of evidence to support such a belief—no background details to add substance to the legend, no consistent account of its usage, and of course no actual flag to be preserved as irrefutable testimony. It is not impossible that some version of the Stars and Stripes did fly over the surrender ceremonies, or was carried in a parade that seventeenth of October, 1777. For example, the distinguished Vermont historian John Spargo has suggested the interesting and reasonable theory that the Saratoga Stars and Stripes was the Bennington Flag.

Captain Dewey's Bennington militia did march to Bemis Heights to assist Gates. And they may have brought with them the proud symbol of their recent victory over Burgoyne's raiding party. Whatever the explanation of the Saratoga flag tradition it is certain that the banner was not an official government or Army flag. No Congressional or military agency had the desire or the money to provide national colors to the ground forces. Almost two full years later Washington was still trying to get colors for his troops. But the Army was not accepting the Stars and Stripes as a battle flag. And the Congress had not assigned the national flag to the military nor had it provided a "standard" for Army usage. On May 10, 1779, the secretary of the Board of War, Richard Peters, wrote to Washington: "It is not yet settled what is the Standard of the U. States. If your Excellency will therefore favor us with your Opinion on the subject we will report to Congress and request them to establish a Standard . . ."

The official reluctance to use the new national flag in the field all but annihilates two other claims to the first unfurling of a "government issue" Stars and Stripes —at Cooch's Bridge, Delaware, on September 3, 1777, and at Brandywine, Pennsylvania, eight days later. Both of these claims are left dangling in the air, unsupported by any contemporary or subsequent evidence.

In the Southern states no known attempt was made to interpret the new flag law for several years. Then on January 17, 1781, the Third Maryland Regiment is believed to have fought at Cowpens, South Carolina, under a starred and striped banner that fulfilled in every detail the first flag resolution. No record exists as to the origin or maker of this unofficial flag. All that is known is that it appeared on that date in Colonel John Eager Howard's regiment carried by the Color Sergeant William Batchelor. The sergeant was wounded during the American victory that day and returned to his Baltimore home bringing the banner with him. The flag was carefully preserved throughout the 1800's and presented to the state of Maryland in 1907. It is now in the Statehouse at Annapolis.

Another flag believed to have been carried by Southern troops at this time is the so-called North Carolina Militia Flag. This flag, now preserved in the Hall of History at Raleigh, has blue and red stripes and thirteen blue stars on a white canton. Its reversed colors may have been based upon a misinterpretation of the flag law. But it seems more likely that the design was selected to provide a distinctive banner for militia. Although some historians have reported that this flag flew at the battle of Guilford Courthouse, March 15, 1781, such an assumption is made on the basis of little or no evidence.

There is a similar lack of evidence to support the theory that a Stars and Stripes flew over the final American triumph at Yorktown. One or more of the starred and striped banners mentioned here might have been hoisted over that historic site—or perhaps some other appropriate emblem that has now been lost forever. Unfortunately, however, all such claims fail to survive the most cursory investigation. It is an established fact that despite repeated requests for national colors the

American commander in chief, George Washington, did not receive such flags until March 1783, more than a year after the end of land combat in the Revolution. Even then the Stars and Stripes was restricted to use on forts, camps, and military establishments. As will be seen later, no Army unit received authorization to carry the national flag as a regimental color (or standard) until 1834.

On land, then, there was no official Stars and Stripes carried in battle during the Revolution. The colorful variations of the Congressional flag resolution, such as the Bennington and Cowpens banners, were personal and unofficial interpretations, not directly descendent from the national legislation but only heraldic "cousins" to it.

At sea there was no such confusion and controversy. Even those who believed the Congress did not intend the "flag of the thirteen United States" to be an Army banner had no such doubts about naval usage. From the very first the young Navy adopted the Stars and Stripes as its official ensign. Although there is an expected amount of folklore and fantasy attendant upon the first marine usage, the record is unmistakably clear—and brilliant enough to obviate legendary embellishments.

The record of flag "firsts" at sea is virtually the story of John Paul Jones's naval exploits. This was a fact that the never modest Jones was quick to realize. According to one biographer, Jones is on record as writing: "The Flag and I are twins; born the same day and the same hour [referring to his appointment by Congress to command of the *Ranger* the same day the flag resolution was adopted]. We cannot be parted in life or in death. So long as we can float, we shall float together. If we must sink, we shall go down as one."

After receiving his orders Jones left Philadelphia to take over the *Ranger* at Portsmouth, reaching that city July 12, 1777. This fact renders absurd the story that on the Fourth of July he hoisted from his ship a Stars and Stripes made by five young Portsmouth ladies "from their best silk dresses." There can be little doubt, however, that Jones was the first to fly the new flag from a naval vessel. The date was on or before November 1, 1777, when Jones sailed the *Ranger* out into the Atlantic, taking the ensign to sea for the first time.

More flag firsts followed in rapid succession. En route to France, the first capture of an enemy vessel was made under the Stars and Stripes. Jones carried the flag to a foreign port (Nantes) for the first time and on February 14, 1778, the new ensign received its first salute from a foreign power. The place was Quiberon Bay, off the coast of Brittany, and the salute was nine guns—the highest number the French Royal Navy could give the flag of a republican power. Two months later in a savage battle in the Irish Sea, the *Ranger,* with eighteen guns, compelled the *Drake,* with twenty guns, to strike its colors to the Stars and Stripes, the first British warship to suffer this humiliation. Proudly Jones wrote to the American commissioner in Paris: "The American stars were displayed on board the *Ranger.*" Aware of Jones's romantic attachment to the flag, one might question the full truth of his claims. But each claim has been substantiated by reliable evidence, especially by the

Washington Coat-of-Arms (page 43)

Easton, Pennsylvania, Flag (page 48)

Bennington Flag (page 62)

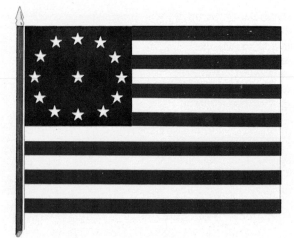

Third Maryland Regiment (page 65)

diary kept by Dr. Ezra Green, surgeon on board the *Ranger*.

Jones's most memorable battle came on September 23, 1779, off Flamborough Head, England, and gave rise to his most famous quote: "I have not yet begun to fight." His ship, the sea-scarred forty-gun *Bonhomme Richard*, was damaged beyond repair in a clash with the British *Serapis* of fifty guns. Pulling alongside the enemy warship the Americans abandoned their sinking vessel and scrambled aboard the subdued *Serapis*. Jones is reputed to have described the final scene: "The very last vestige mortal eyes ever saw of the *Bonhomme Richard* was the defiant waving of her unconquered and unstricken Flag as she went down. And as I had given them the good old ship for their sepulchre, I now bequeathed to my immortal dead the Flag they had so desperately defended, for their winding sheet."

Strangely enough, this episode served as the springboard for one of the most ingenious of flag legends. A supposedly authentic *Bonhomme Richard* flag was later acquired by the Congress and presented to James Stafford, a seaman who reportedly served under Jones aboard the *Bonhomme Richard*. According to Stafford's story, he had rescued and rehoisted the ensign after it had been cut down during the battle. This flag has but twelve stars in the canton, arranged in four rows of three stars each. One version of the story says that a thirteenth star stood apart from the others near the hoist of the flag. This star is said to have been cut from the flag and sent to President Lincoln during the Civil War! To avoid contradicting Jones's testimony of the sinking of the ship—and flag—it was alleged that the Stafford flag was not the ensign of the *Bonhomme Richard* but a second Stars and Stripes which was transferred to the *Serapis* at the conclusion of the battle. This flag was displayed for a time in the Smithsonian Institution but was removed from exhibition when its authenticity was seriously questioned. Careful examination indicated that it was really a fifteen-star, fifteen-stripe flag of the era 1795–1818 with the top row of three stars and the two top stripes removed. Such a flag, of course, postdated the *Bonhomme Richard* by sixteen years!

In addition to the *Ranger* and the *Bonhomme Richard,* Jones also sailed the *Alliance* and the *Ariel* under the Stars and Stripes. Because none of these ensigns have been preserved, their exact configuration is in doubt. Early interpretations of the first flag law varied in the Navy as elsewhere. One eyewitness account of Jones's flags describes a canton of thirteen eight-pointed stars and a field of red, white, and *blue* stripes. This is the flag sketched in the shipping office of the Dutch port of Texel, where Jones's fleet found refuge after the crippling battle with the *Serapis.*

The fighting men of the American Revolution were not the only ones responsible for the colorful variations in the early Stars and Stripes. Even America's two most distinguished diplomats of the time, Benjamin Franklin and John Adams, misinterpreted the flag law. In a letter sent from Paris, October 9, 1778, they wrote (or at least jointly signed the letter): ". . . the flag of the United States of America consists of 13 stripes, alternately red, white, and blue; a small square in the upper angle, next the flag staff, is a blue field, with 13 stars, denoting a new Constellation."

Confusion as to the precise form of the new national flag was to last for many years. As late as 1847 the Dutch government was bewildered by the wide and numerous variations in the Stars and Stripes. Through diplomatic channels it politely inquired as to just what was the official pattern and style of the American ensign.

CHAPTER 6

★ ★ ★ ★ ★

★ ★ ★ ★ ★

"A MORE PERFECT UNION"

The victory at Yorktown ended the long struggle for independence that had begun as a local insurrection in New England more than six years before. Along the seaboard the last skirmish occurred at Combahee River, South Carolina, on August 27, 1782, and by the end of the year the British had evacuated all the Atlantic ports except New York, from which they withdrew several months later. Formal peace negotiations in Paris produced a preliminary treaty, effective January 20, 1783, and a final treaty signed eight months later. American negotiators won such favorable terms that the French minister Vergennes was astounded. The new United States was off to a good start with the Stars and Stripes taking its place among the national flags of the world.

At home the American people struggled to erect an

orderly government under the Articles of Confederation and Perpetual Union that had gone into effect March 1, 1781. During these crucial formative years the uncertainty of the times was reflected in the frequent moving of the national capital. From 1783 to 1785 the flag over the Capitol was hoisted in five different cities—Philadelphia, Princeton, Annapolis, Trenton, and New York. It was in Annapolis, under a banner of thirteen stars and thirteen stripes in the Statehouse, that General Washington appeared before "The United States in Congress Assembled" in 1783 to resign his commission as commander in chief and take "leave of all the employments of public life." Under the same flag, in the same room, the Annapolis Convention of 1786 (five states represented) met to discuss interstate commerce and instead issued a call for all the states to send delegates to a convention scheduled for Philadelphia the following year.

The new convention was to consider all matters necessary "to render the constitution of the Federal Government adequate to the exigencies of the Union." It was high time for action. According to one observer, the young nation was "floundering helplessly in a sea of unpaid debts and broken promises." A severe depression had been aggravated by the financial follies of the federal and various state governments. Paper money had become so cheap that it gave rise to the enduring phrase "not worth a continental." In 1786–1787 the general unrest in the nation exploded into armed rebellion in Massachusetts when Daniel Shays, a Revolutionary War captain, led a mob of debt-ridden rural followers in an attack upon the state government.

At the height of political and economic discontent the Constitutional Convention assembled in Philadelphia's Statehouse, May 25, 1787. For the next four months— perhaps the most critical period in the nation's history —fifty-five farseeing delegates labored to hammer out a new system of government. The success of their efforts is apparent to all the world today.

The new Constitution was ratified in 1788 and began to function the following April when the first Congress convened and Washington took the oath of office as the first President. At last the Stars and Stripes was on certain ground. (The Bill of Rights, or first ten amendments to the Constitution, went into effect two years later.)

The only efforts to add a new state to the union during the 1780's met with failure. In 1784 the trans-Allegheny settlers of North Carolina, led by John Sevier, held a convention at Jonesboro (now in Tennessee) and set up the independent state of Franklin, or Frankland. Despite a clamor for admission, the federal government ignored the frontier organization and it collapsed four years later. Thus, a possible change in the national flag's symbolism of thirteen was postponed for another ten years.

During this time the Stars and Stripes was gaining recognition and respect all over the globe. On February 3, 1783, Captain William Mooers, out of Nantucket, sailed the *Bedford* up the Thames to London, a peacetime first not unnoticed in England. A London paper reported: "This is the first vessel which has displayed the thirteen rebellious stripes of America in any British port." And thirteen equally rebellious stars, it might have added.

The new American ensign reached the Orient for the first time on August 30, 1784, when Captain John Greene, sailing out of New York, navigated the *Empress of China* into port at Canton. His return cargo of tea and silks brought such handsome profits that merchants along the Atlantic seaboard quickly fitted out other ships for the China trade.

Probably the best job of publicizing the Stars and Stripes during this period was done by a Rhode Island naval captain, Robert Gray. Out of Boston, September 30, 1787, he carried the flag to Nootka Sound in the *Lady Washington*. Transferring his ensign to the *Columbia*, he sailed around the world in that ship, returning to Boston in August, 1790. Two years later Gray sailed up the mouth of the great river of Oregon, renaming it in honor of the *Columbia*.

The Bostonians, who had led the long fight against British rule, could take special pride in another historic incident. On May 2, 1791, the *Alligator*, commanded by Captain Isaac Coffin, sailed into Boston harbor, the first British man-of-war to enter an American port since the Revolution. The warship rendered a thirteen-gun salute to the bright flag flying atop Fort Independence (then Castle William) and received a similar salute in return.

What did these pioneering national flags look like? Unfortunately, few actual banners have survived and most contemporary records omit detailed descriptions of the national ensign of this period. It is certain, however, that there was little uniformity in these early flags. The resolution of 1777 left too many questions unanswered. What were to be the proportions of the flag? And the proportions of its parts? Were the stripes to be horizontal or vertical? How were the stars to be arranged? And of what design? Even the basic text of the first law had received but little circulation. In an effort to obtain some uniformity of design the *Pennsylvania Gazette* of April 23, 1783, reprinted the flag resolution in full and added this plea: "The Printers in the several States are requested to insert the above Resolution in their respective News-papers in order that the same may be generally known."

Under the circumstances it is surprising that the flag had any uniformity at all. Although there were many exceptions the stars and stripes were usually made in pleasing proportions not unlike the legal dimensions prescribed today. A horizontal direction of the stripes was also commonly accepted. Here the Grand Union provided a distinguished tradition. Some writers have sought to show that the vertical stripes of the Coast Guard ensign, adopted in 1799, indicated a frequency of such markings on the national flag. But it seems more reasonable that the contrary was true. Vertical stripes were chosen to achieve a distinctive emblem for the Coast Guard (then called the Revenue Marine Service).

Thus, only in the design and arrangement of stars did the flag vary considerably. Originally, flag makers constructed stars with eight, seven, six, or five points. The designs came from various sources. Eight-pointed stars were commonly sewn on bed quilts, and both six-

Fort Independence flag

and five-pointed stars existed in heraldry (usually six in England, and five on the Continent). The so-called Fort Independence flag had five-pointed stars arranged in three horizontal rows. This flag was made for Jonathan Fowle of Boston in 1781. It flew over Castle William in Boston harbor, where Fowle's son was a member of the garrison. It is now preserved in the Statehouse at Boston.

One of the earliest Army colors, that of the First Infantry of 1791, had eight-pointed stars.[1] (So had the Easton flag; the Bennington banner had seven.) The stars on other Army flags varied from seven to five. By the time of the War of 1812, however, the stars on most Army flags had become six-pointed; and with the coming of the Mexican War almost all colors and standards contained stars with five points. There is little evidence

[1] For national colors during this time the Army carried a blue flag charged with an eagle in the center. Below the eagle was a scroll designating the unit. Above the eagle were the stars, one for each state in the Union. The Army did not wait for changes in the Stars and Stripes. It added one star to its national colors each time a new state was admitted.

to show how the stars were arranged on post and garrison flags. Perhaps the most significant clue is the War Office seal designed in 1778. This device contains (among other things) two flags. One is a plain banner without markings, evidently intended as a regimental color; the other is the Stars and Stripes, with the thirteen stars arranged in three horizontal rows. It would be a mistake, however, to conclude that all Stars and Stripes used by the Army followed this pattern. Most of the flags of the Army and of government agencies were made by private contractors who took considerable latitude in designing and arranging the stars.

Navy flag

The Navy, on the other hand, manufactured its own flags and soon settled upon rows of stars arranged 3-2-3-2-3. This design of the combined crosses of St. George and St. Andrew became the most popular method of placing the stars in the canton of naval flags until the addition of two stars in 1795 rendered the old arrangement impractical.

One of the many misapprehensions about the first Stars and Stripes is that the stars were commonly arranged in a circle. This arrangement was allegedly chosen so that no state would have preference over any other. Yet the idea of assigning a particular star to a certain state (an illogical practice that has never been officially sanctioned) did not arise until much later.

There is no evidence to show that the circular arrangement of stars was ever popular. One flag bearing this design is in the Fort Ticonderoga Museum, but proof of the banner's authenticity rests upon highly questionable evidence. It was supposedly made by the ubiquitous Betsy Ross to fulfill an order placed by General Philip Schuyler before June 14, 1777. Schuyler had left Philadelphia for Albany the first week in June; so, in order to match the flag with established fact, it was postulated that Schuyler knew of the resolution before it was adopted. This seems extremely doubtful.

The starry-circle legend has developed chiefly from popular paintings, which were composed with little regard for historical accuracy. Among the earliest paintings showing the circle arrangement are Charles W. Peale's portraits of Washington at Trenton and at Valley Forge. Two other examples, both painted much later, are A. M. Willard's "The Spirit of '76" and Emanuel Leutze's "Washington Crossing the Delaware." Another influencing factor may have been the pleasant fiction, "Birth of Our Nation's Flag," a painting by Charles H. Weisgerber, which shows Betsy Ross displaying what is supposed to be the first Stars and Stripes.

The foremost painter of the Revolution, John Trumbull, recorded a quite different arrangement of stars. In his wartime scenes at Princeton (which predated the flag law by six months), Saratoga, and Yorktown he showed the national flag with twelve stars in a hollow square and the thirteenth in the center.

If there was any controversy over how the stars were to be arranged in this first Stars and Stripes, it was short-lived. Vermont had been admitted to the Union in 1791 and Kentucky the following year. Both states were now clamoring for representation in the national flag.

★ ★ ★ ★ ★   FIRST TEN REPRODUCTIONS OF THE STARS AND STRIPES

During the early 1780's the first engraved representations of the Stars and Stripes began to appear. As the following illustrations show, there was scant uniformity of design in these pioneering cuts. In fact only two of the ten reproduce the flag in accordance with the law of June 14, 1777—Abel Buell (number 4) and Francis Bailey (number 5).

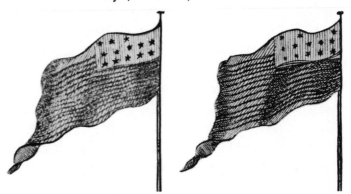

1 and 2. Probably the first American illustration of the national flag was contained in *Weatherwise's Town and Country Almanack,* published at Boston, October 4, 1781. The compiler was David Rittenhouse, who took the pseudonym Abraham Weatherwise in putting out a series of almanacs between 1781 and 1790. The plate displaying the Stars and Stripes is found in two issues, both carrying a six-part illustration of "America Triumphant and Britannica in Distress." Each flag has thirteen stars but one has fourteen stripes and the other fifteen.

3. Abroad, the earliest known reproduction, also in 1781, is carried in a flag sheet published at Paris by Mondhare. As "the newest of the world's *pavillons,*" the Stars and Stripes of the "American Congress" is shown in the bottom row. It has the correct number of seven red and six white stripes. In the canton, however, the thirteenth star is represented by a fleur-de-lis. Following the national flag, and likewise in color, are three other American emblems: (1) the mercantile flag of the United States of America—thirteen alternate red and white stripes; (2) a naval pennant—two broad horizontal stripes of red and white; and (3) another naval banner in the shape of the present commission pennant—again with twelve stars and one fleur-de-lis.

4. Abel Buell's "A New and Correct Map of the United States" was advertised for subscription at New Haven, March 31, 1784. For heraldic purposes, the most notable feature is the correct reproduction of the Stars and Stripes, which is made a part of an elaborate cartouche in the lower right hand corner of the map. Made "agreeable to the peace of 1783," the map measures 41 by 46 inches. In Buell's own words it was "the first ever compiled, engraved, and finished by one man, and an American."

5. The only other correct representation of the flag in this series was part of a tiny flag sheet incorporated in *Bailey's Pocket Almanac*, published at Philadelphia in the fall of 1784. Shown in black and white, the colors are correctly identified by a key accompanying the engraving. The full title of the publication was *Bailey's Pocket Almanac, being an American Annual Register*

*for the Year of our Lord 1785; and of the empire the
tenth. The first after Bissextile (Leap Year).* It was one
of a series of annual almanacs (6¾ inches high) put out
through 1790 by Francis Bailey at Yorick's Head in
Market Street, Philadelphia.

6. After the 1782 signing of the preliminary articles of
peace between the United States and Great Britain,
John Wallis of London published a map of "The United
States of America," April 3, 1783. The map was "laid
down from the best Authorities Agreeable to the Peace
of 1783." Fortunately for Wallis this provisional agreement became the definitive peace treaty five months
later. Wallis's representation of the American flag re-
verses the white and red stripes, putting a white stripe
at the top and bottom in accordance with the technical
rules of heraldry (following page).

THE UNITED STATES of AMERICA laid down From the best Authorities, Agreeable to the Peace of — 1783. — Published April 3.ᵈ 1783, by the Proprietor JOHN WALLIS, at his Map-Warehouse, Ludgate Street, LONDON

7. A flag with red, white, and blue stripes was illustrated in color by a Leipzig publisher, Matthias Sprengel, in 1784. It was contained in his *Allgemeines historisches Taschenbuch . . . (Pocketbook of World History . . .).* The book carried both the flag and pennant of the "13 sovereign states of North America." In referring to the illustrations Sprengel made the interesting prophecy that this new heraldic device would soon become much more widely known (page 89). In eleven other engravings the highlights of the American Revolution were traced from the Sugar Act of 1764 through the British evacuation of New York in 1783.

North Carolina Militia (page 66)

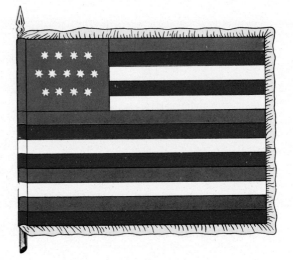

John Paul Jones Texel Flag (page 72)

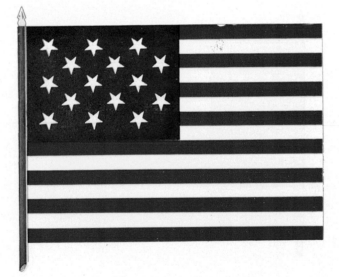

DONT GIVE UP THE SHIP

Perry's Lake Erie Flag (page 96)

The Star-Spangled Banner (page 98)

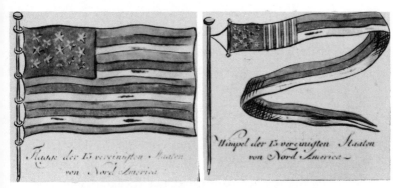

Flagge der 13 vereinigten Staaten von Nord America

Wimpel der 13 vereinigten Staaten von Nord America

8. Another early German reproduction of the flag was contained in a flag sheet by Matthaeus Seutter. Published by Tobias Conrad Lotter at Augsburg, the sheet is undated. Like the Mondhare engraving it shows a fleur-de-lis in the canton. But unlike the French illustration Seutter portrays the full complement of thirteen stars.

XIII Prov. von America

9. An indistinct Stars and Stripes is shown in an aquatint, "Lady Harriet Ackland (Acland)." It is clear, however, that the flag carries too many stripes. Published in London on November 15, 1784, the engraving is by Robert Pollard, the aquatint by Francis Jukes. Lady Ackland and her party are shown in an open boat approaching an American outpost on the banks of the Hudson River. The lady is "delivering herself into the hands of the enemy" to attend her husband who was wounded and captured at Saratoga, October 7, 1777. A companion holds a flag of truce.

10. Soon after the climactic victory at Yorktown, Sebastian Bauman's plan of the siege was engraved and printed at Philadelphia (probably early in 1782). Here again the white and red stripes of the flag have been reversed. Although it is sometimes claimed that the Stars and Stripes flew above Washington's encampment at Yorktown, there is no contemporary proof that the

flag was actually displayed there. One source often cited is John Trumbull's painting of the surrender. This portrayal was not finished until 1797, however, and was painted from memory in London.

CHAPTER 7

THE STAR-SPANGLED BANNER

"*Be it enacted,* That from and after the first day of May, anno domini one thousand seven hundred and ninety-five, the flag of the United States be fifteen stripes, alternate red and white. That the Union be fifteen stars, white in a blue field." With these words the third Congress, sitting at Philadelphia in 1794, amended the nation's first Stars and Stripes to give representation to the two states lately admitted to the Union—Vermont and Kentucky.

In contrast to the first flag law, which had passed without debate, the new bill found surprisingly strong opposition in the House of Representatives. The measure was first introduced into the Senate on December 26, 1793, by Stephen R. Bradley, the first senior senator from Vermont. Four days later it was passed without comment and sent to the House. Here it aroused a storm

of protest. George Thacher of Massachusetts ridiculed the measure as "a consummate piece of frivolity." Israel Smith of Vermont deplored the great expense that a new flag would entail. He said that it would cost him personally five hundred dollars and every vessel in the Union sixty dollars.

The severest critic of the bill was Benjamin Goodhue of Massachusetts, who considered it a "trifling" measure. Peering into the future Goodhue boldly predicted that in the course of years the nation might have twenty states and therefore twenty stars to consider for the flag. Obviously a never-ending chore for Congress, and too many symbols to crowd upon a single flag.

The proponents of the bill were less vocal and more patient. They waited until the opposition had had its say and then passed the measure January 8, 1794, by a vote of fifty to forty-two. President Washington signed it into law five days later.

This new Stars and Stripes was the flag of the first five Presidents—Washington, John Adams, Jefferson,

Madison, and Monroe. It was also the flag of two amendments to the Constitution—the eleventh, ratified in 1798, which declared that a state cannot be sued by citizens of another state; and the twelfth, ratified in 1804, which required separate electoral ballots for President and vice-president. Under the flag of fifteen, five states were admitted to the union, although none received immediate representation in the flag itself—Tennessee (1796), Ohio (1803, but not technically admitted until 1953), Louisiana (1812), Indiana (1816), and Mississippi (1817).

During the administration of President John Adams the second Stars and Stripes served nobly during an undeclared naval war with France. It was this troubled affair that produced Charles C. Pinckney's ringing declaration of American foreign policy: "Millions for defense but not one cent for tribute." It was also during this time that the still-young nation launched its first peacetime warships—the *United States*, the *Constellation*, and the *Constitution*. With a succession of Stars and Stripes as their ensigns, these three frigates helped make the United States second only to Great Britain as a naval power during their long periods of sea duty. The *Constellation* served until 1854; the *United States* until 1861, when it was destroyed by Union forces as they evacuated Norfolk during the first year of the Civil War; and the *Constitution* until 1878. The latter, popularly called "Old Ironsides," is now preserved in the Boston Naval Yard.

Three different banners of fifteen stars and fifteen stripes flew over historic milestones in the expansion of the nation. The national flag was raised over the national Capitol in Washington, D.C., for the first time on November 17, 1800, as Congress convened for its inaugural session in this building. On December 20, 1803, at New Orleans, the French flag was hauled down in the Place d'Armes and the Stars and Stripes hoisted in its place. The vast territory of Louisiana was now American soil at a cost of only fifteen million dollars. The following spring Meriwether Lewis and William Clark began their ascent of the Missouri River. On their long journey to the mouth of the Columbia, Lewis and Clark became the first to carry the Stars and Stripes across the continent. The United States had won the race to the Pacific.

Abroad, bold Americans requested and received new recognition for their national banner in the Old World. In 1800 Captain William Bainbridge in the frigate *George Washington* carried the Stars and Stripes through the Bosporus to the walls of Constantinople (now Istanbul). The surprised sultan knew nothing of either the flag or the nation it represented. After hearing the Americans' explanation that they were from the new world discovered by Columbus, the Turks sent aboard a bunch of flowers to show welcome and a lamp as an expression of amity.

Five years later an undeclared war against the Barbary pirates came to an end when Marine Lieutenant O'Bannon and Midshipman Mann hauled down the Tripolitan colors over the fortress of Derne (now Derna in Libya). The Stars and Stripes that they ran to the top of the flagpole was the first such banner to fly over any of the fortresses erected in the Old World.

In 1812 the continuing friction between Great Britain and America on the seas finally flared into formal warfare. Before President Madison proclaimed the war declaration on June 19, a secret council in Washington, D.C., determined to keep American warships out of the forthcoming conflict. The council was unwilling to risk its few frigates and sloops (with a total of only 412 guns) in an uneven contest against the powerful British navy. Fortunately this despairing order was quickly revoked, due chiefly to the protests of two courageous captains—William Bainbridge and Charles Stewart. The thumping naval victories turned in by American naval commanders during the next two years proved that Bainbridge and Stewart had not been indulging in idle heroics. Chief among these engagements were the capture of the British frigate *Guerrière* by Isaac Hull in the *Constitution;* the capture of the *Macedonian* by Stephen Decatur in the *United States;* the defeat of the *Java* by William Bainbridge, then commanding the *Constitution;* Oliver Hazard Perry's squadron victory on Lake Erie ("We have met the enemy and they are ours"); and Thomas MacDonough's sweep of Lake Champlain in the battle of Plattsburg.

One of the worst naval disasters suffered by the United States in this war was the loss of the *Chesapeake* to the *Shannon* (after the dying words of Captain James Lawrence: "Don't give up the ship"). Three months after this defeat, on September 10, 1813, at Put-in-Bay, Lake Erie, Master Commandant O. H. Perry hoisted a special flag from the mainmast of his flagship, the *Law-*

rence. On a blue field was lettered in white the dead captain's order, "Don't Give Up the Ship." When the *Lawrence* was lost in the battle, Perry transferred his flag to the *Niagara* and from this vessel directed the decisive victory over the British fleet. His unique battle flag is now preserved in the Naval Academy Museum.

Army national color (1803-1812)

On land the Army still did not carry the Stars and Stripes but rather its own distinctive national colors of blue, featuring the American eagle surmounted by white stars. This was the banner that flew at the Thames River (Ontario) in 1813, when General Harrison crushed the menace of the Northwest Territory Indians; at Bladensburg in 1814, when the Americans abandoned the city of Washington; and at New Orleans in 1815, when Andrew Jackson overwhelmed the British attackers two weeks after the peace treaty had been signed at Ghent.

Regimental flag (War of 1812)

For all its valiant service during the twenty-three years of its existence the second Stars and Stripes is best remembered for its role at Fort McHenry during the British land and naval attack on Baltimore, September 12–14, 1814. The Fort McHenry flag, measuring thirty by forty-two feet, had been made for the garrison by Mrs. Mary Pickersgill, of Baltimore, and her daughter. The needlework had earned the seamstresses $405.90, presumably paid by Colonel George Armistead, commander of the fort.

When the British opened their attack on Fort McHenry, a young American lawyer, Francis Scott Key, was aboard the British warship *Minden*. He had gone to the fleet commander to plead for the release of a captured friend, Dr. William Beanes. His request had been granted but he was detained by the British during the attack. Throughout the day and night of September 13, 1814, British guns bombarded the fort. Fearing the attack would succeed, Key paced the deck of the ship all night. Finally, as it grew light on the morning of the fourteenth, Key's anxious eyes spotted the gallant flag still waving above Fort McHenry. The sight inspired him to write the verses of "The Star-Spangled Banner," officially adopted as the national anthem in 1931. The flag, with eleven holes shot in it, was presented to the Smithsonian Institution in 1912 by Eben Appleton, grandson of the fort's successful defender, Colonel Armistead.

In the original Star-Spangled Banner the stars are five-pointed and arranged in five staggered rows of three stars each. A similar arrangement is found in the ensign of the captured *Chesapeake,* now in the Royal United Service Institution in London. The ensign of the *Enterprise,* which defeated the *Boxer* off the coast of Maine in 1813, is preserved in the Smithsonian Institution. Although only eight of the original stars remain they show a definite linear arrangement.

Another surviving flag of the era is the ensign that flew over Stonington, Connecticut, during the British bombardment of August 9–10, 1814. Its unknown designer, taking considerable liberty with the flag law of 1795, fashioned a banner with sixteen stripes and sixteen stars arranged in four even rows of four each. This would presumably date the flag sometime between 1796 (the admission of Tennessee) and 1803 (when Ohio entered the Union). Carried by the local militia unit, the Eighth Company of the Thirtieth Connecticut Regiment, it was nailed to the pole during the British attack to forestall any idea of lowering it in surrender. The flag is now preserved in the Old Stone Bank in Stonington.

An exception to this linear arrangement of stars is

the crude banner that flew over Fort Hill, Maine, during the War of 1812. In this flag the stars are scattered over the canton in no recognizable order. This flag is now in the Smithsonian Institution.

Fort Hill flag

The flag of fifteen stars and fifteen stripes flew for twenty-three years and two months, longer than any other Stars and Stripes except the twenty-fifth, which served from 1912 to 1959. In one respect, however, the second Stars and Stripes holds a unique place in history. As the inspiration for "The Star-Spangled Banner," it is the only flag in the world to be the subject of a national anthem.

CHAPTER 8

★ ★ ★ ★ ★

★ ★ ★ ★ ★

A PERMANENT FLAG LAW

Many men and women have received credit for their contributions to the development of the Stars and Stripes. Some of the credit has been deserved. Too often it has been misplaced or misrepresented. On the other hand, the two men most deserving of recognition are generally overlooked. Yet their work produced the flag law that has been in force since July 4, 1818. The men: Peter Wendover and Samuel Reid.

Soon after the War of 1812 it became apparent that the flag law of 1795 would have to be amended. Each of the first fifteen states in the union was represented in the national flag by a star and a stripe. But now Tennessee had been a state since 1796 and had received no recognition in the national ensign. Ohio, Louisiana, and Indiana had also been admitted without representation. Mississippi was preparing for statehood and others were to follow it in rapid succession.

In 1816, Wendover, a first-term congressman from New York, persuaded the House that legislative action was necessary. He got himself appointed chairman of a special committee to study the flag problem. It was obvious that the practice of adding one stripe and one star for each new state would not do. The flag would soon look like a strip of peppermint shirting, and the stripes would become increasingly narrow until they were little more than lines. Wendover wanted to retain the distinctive character of the flag, yet make it a truly national banner. He sought the advice of Captain Samuel Reid, a naval hero of the War of 1812. Reid proved to be an excellent consultant. He advised reducing the number of stripes to thirteen, one for each of the original thirteen states, and then placing one star in the canton for each state in the Union. Whenever a new state was admitted, one more star would be added to the flag.

Wendover liked the idea. A bill was drawn up and reported to the House of Representatives. Although Wendover urged immediate enactment, the fourteenth Congress adjourned before the measure could be considered. Undiscouraged, the New York representative renewed his efforts in the fifteenth Congress, which convened in December, 1817. In support of his pet project Wendover pointed out the great variety of existing flags. On one wing of the Capitol was flying a flag with thirteen stars and thirteen stripes. On other public buildings in Washington were displayed at least three other variations of the Stars and Stripes, only one of which was authorized—a flag of fifteen stars and fifteen stripes. One banner had been made up in June, 1788, after New Hampshire's ratification (the ninth state) had ensured the adoption of the new Constitution. It had but nine stars and nine stripes. Another had given unauthorized recognition to Tennessee, Ohio, and Louisiana by creating a flag of eighteen stars and eighteen stripes.

When Wendover's bill reached the floor of the House it was beset by three alternative suggestions. Walter Folger, Jr., of Massachusetts proposed to restore the original flag of thirteen stars and thirteen stripes, adopted in 1777. George Poindexter of Mississippi had a similar plan. He would reduce the number of stripes to thirteen and then place seven stars in the canton for the states that had entered the Union after the original thirteen. The oddest idea of all came from George Robertson of Kentucky. For no apparent reason he suggested an arbitrary number of stars and stripes such as nine or eleven. Fortunately, all these motions were rejected by big majorities and Wendover's bill passed the House, March 25, 1818, with only a few dissenting votes. In its final form the bill was "An Act to Establish the Flag of the United States." It read:

Section 1. Be it enacted, That from and after the fourth day of July next, the flag of the United States be thirteen horizontal stripes, alternate red and white; that the union have twenty stars, white in a blue field.

Section 2. And be it further enacted, That on the admission of every new State into the Union, one star be added to the union of the flag; and that such addition

A Permanent Flag Law ★ 103

shall take effect on the fourth of July next succeeding such admission.

The Senate passed the bill unanimously and President Monroe signed it into law, April 4, 1818. For the first time the stripes in the national flag were legally established as horizontal. There was, however, no provision for the arrangement of the stars. This was deliberate. In a speech to the House on March 24, Wendover had suggested that the arrangement of stars be "left to the discretion of persons more immediately concerned, either to arrange them in the form of one great luminary or in the words of the original resolution of 1777, representing a new constellation."

Congress was so proud of its heraldic handiwork it could not wait the three months it required of the rest of the nation. On April 13 it had hoisted above the Capitol the new flag of twenty stars and thirteen stripes. The flag, made by Mrs. Samuel Reid, had the stars arranged in the form of one "great luminary."

Mrs. Reid's method of displaying the stars was not accidental. Her husband favored the large, five-pointed star design "whose brilliancy should represent their [the states'] union and thus symbolize, in the flag, the origin and progress of the country and its motto 'E Pluribus Unum.'" Reid had suggested to Congressman Wendover that for the Army, merchant vessels, federal buildings, and general use on land the stars should be formed into one great star. For Navy warships, he recommended that the stars be arranged in horizontal rows. This distinction was infrequently observed and soon abandoned by the Army and all other government

Texas Lone Star Flag (page 117)

California Bear Flag (page 124)

Bonnie Blue Flag (page 137)

First Confederate Flag (page 138)

agencies, which preferred to make no rulings whatsoever. The Navy was more circumspect. In a directive dated May 18, and amended September 18, 1818, it established that the stars in the canton should be placed in uniform rows. It also ordered that all naval banners should be sized in the proportions fourteen (hoist) by twenty-four (fly); the canton, seven-thirteenths depth of hoist and one-third of fly. This was the first governmental attempt to establish uniformity in the national flag.

Captain Reid had one idea that was far out of line with his other sensible suggestions. Together with Wendover he worked out a "national standard" that was little more than an inept imitation of Great Britain's royal standard. Designed for use by Congress and the President and for federal arsenals and naval yards, it would be divided into four quarters. The first quarter—twenty white stars on blue; second quarter—the eagle of the Great Seal on white; third quarter—the goddess of Liberty on white; and fourth quarter—thirteen alternate red and white stripes. Fortunately this proposal never received serious consideration.

Samuel Chester Reid (1783–1861) lived to see the United States grow from twenty states to thirty-four, each new admission recorded automatically by a star in the canton of the national flag. In 1859 Congress voted its thanks to the aging captain for his enduring contribution to the Stars and Stripes. At that time there was agitation to adopt a uniform method of arranging the stars but Congress failed to take any action. (As a matter of fact Congress has never seen fit to do so; the arrangement, changing when a new state is admitted, is determined by an executive order of the President.)

Peter Hercules Wendover (1768–1834) had held several local offices in New York City and had been a state representative before his election to Congress in 1814. A Democrat, he was twice re-elected before retiring to become sheriff of New York County for three years. Except for his untiring crusade to establish a permanent national flag, Wendover passed unnoticed into history.

★ ★ ★ ★ ★   U.S.A. FLAG 1818–1819

In contrast to the first two official national flags, which served eighteen and twenty-three years respectively, the third Stars and Stripes was in existence only twelve months. Within that single year, however, the nation took two long steps toward determining what were to be its permanent national boundaries. On October 20, 1818, the forty-ninth parallel, from the Lake of the Woods west to the Rocky

Mountains, was established as the border between the United States and Canada. Then four months later Spain tired of General Andrew Jackson's bullying tactics in the Floridas and agreed to cede both the east and west sections to the United States.

Meanwhile Illinois, which had been a slow-growing territory since 1809, now pushed hard for statehood, and made it on December 3, 1818. But only because both the territorial government and Congress were willing to wink at federal regulations. Illinois's population was only 40,258, almost 20,000 short of the minimum set by the Northwest Ordinance of 1787. And the Illinois convention ratified the new state constitution without submitting it to popular vote. Then came the real coup. Nathaniel Pope, territorial delegate in Congress, set up the state enabling act so that the northern boundary was moved from the tip of Lake Michigan to a point sixty miles farther north (to 42° 31′). This bit of territory, virtually stolen from what later became Wisconsin, now contains well over half the population of the entire state.

CHAPTER 9

★ ★ ★ ★ ★

★ ★ ★ ★ ★

FROM THE ATLANTIC
TO THE PACIFIC

The first automatic addition of a star to the flag took place July 4, 1819, during President Monroe's first administration. Congressman Wendover and adviser Reid had done their work well. The new flag law soon proved to be a happy and practicable heraldic arrangement for a rapidly expanding nation. Within a generation there would be states bordering both the Atlantic and the Pacific. And in less than a hundred years the number of states in the Union would more than double. Yet each new entry received such prompt and appropriate recognition in the flag that the Stars and Stripes was at all times a truly national banner.

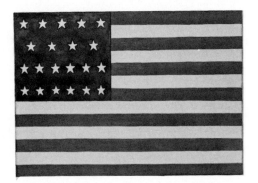

★ ★ ★ ★ ★ U.S.A. FLAG 1819–1820

The twenty-first star, for Illinois, was added to the national flag July 4, 1819. As in the case of the third Stars and Stripes this banner served only one year. But it was a year heavy with the first thunderclaps of antagonism between North and South over the expansion of slavery into the territories. Alabama entered the Union December 14, 1819, providing the eleventh slave state to match the number of free states already admitted. But then Maine began asking for admission, thereby threatening the delicate balance between North and South in the Senate of the United States. At the same time Senator Jesse B. Thomas of Illinois proposed that with the exception of Missouri no new slave states could be created out of the Louisiana Purchase territory north of 36° 30' (the southern boundary of Missouri Territory). After much political jockeying Congress voted to accept Maine as a free state, Missouri as a slave state, and the Thomas amendment as the future dividing line between free and slave states. This legislation, the famous Missouri Compromise, preserved a fragile, uneasy peace between North and South for another generation.

Missouri's actual admission was delayed another seventeen months because of a dispute over discriminatory provisions in its state constitution. Thus by July 4, 1820, only Alabama and Maine (admitted March 15, 1820) had become qualified for representation in the Stars and Stripes.

★ ★ ★ ★ ★   U.S.A. FLAG 1820–1822

When the twenty-second and twenty-third stars were added to the flag for Alabama and Maine, July 4, 1820, it was only the second time two states received simultaneous recognition in the national flag. Vermont and Kentucky had secured dual recognition in 1795. The flag received no other double entry until 1912 when stars were added for both New Mexico and Arizona.

On December 6, 1820, the nation re-elected James

Monroe, its fifth President, with 231 electoral votes. The United States liked the "era of good feeling." The defeated candidate, John Quincy Adams, received a grand total of one electoral vote (from New Hampshire).

In 1821 occurred three apparently unrelated events: (1) Spanish authorities certified a grant of land in Texas for settlement by Moses Austin; (2) Mexico proclaimed its independence from Spain; and (3) William Becknell left Independence, Missouri, with the first wagon train of goods to travel the Santa Fe trail. Although these incidents attracted little attention at the time, their effect was to set in motion a chain reaction that would result in war and eventually propel the western boundary of the nation from the Sabine River to the Pacific and add to the Union six new states and parts of two others.

Meanwhile a second Missouri Compromise was finally agreed upon by both Congress and the legislature of the future "Show Me" state. The Missouri legislature promised by "solemn public act" never to abridge the constitutional rights of citizens of other states—i.e., free Negroes—by enforcing the disputed restrictive clause in its state constitution, which it stubbornly refused to amend. A patent absurdity, but it worked. President Monroe admitted Missouri to the Union by proclamation on August 10, 1821.

★ ★ ★ ★ ★   U.S.A. FLAG 1822–1836

The addition of the twenty-fourth star to the flag, for Missouri, signaled the advent of fourteen

colorful but troubled years under one banner. Now President Monroe's second term was coming to an end and, like Washington, Jefferson, and Madison, he had no wish for a third. In 1824 John Quincy Adams was elected the sixth President of the United States in a tight, four-way struggle with Henry Clay, William Crawford, and Andrew Jackson—a struggle that ended with the House of Representatives choosing the President. (The Tennessee legislature set some sort of record for eagerness the following year by again nominating Jackson for the Presidency). Except for the Tariff of Abominations enacted in 1828, Adams's administration passed quietly. Seeking re-election, he was defeated by his strongest rival of four years before—Andrew Jackson. The election of the stormy, sandy-haired Tennessean ended twenty-eight consecutive years of Democratic-Republican rule. It also initiated the era of Jacksonian Democracy. Although Jackson did not singlehandedly create this period of social revolt and humanitarianism, he did become its outstanding champion. And he established beyond recall the principle that the American government is the servant of the people's will.

Before leaving office President Monroe extended the protection of the Stars and Stripes to all independent republics of the Western Hemisphere. On December 2, 1823, the President's annual message to Congress outlined the historic Monroe Doctrine, a cornerstone of the United States foreign policy still in effect today. The fifth President stated that "the American continents . . . are henceforth not to be considered as subjects for future colonization by any European power." At the same time he promised noninterference by America in European affairs. Any infringement of this policy was to be viewed "as the manifestation of an unfriendly disposition toward the United States." The following year Russia agreed to limit its southern expansion along the Pacific coast to 54° 40′—a geographic delineation that was to become so charged with emotion in twenty years that it would help elect a President.

The flag of twenty-four stars was the original "Old Glory." In 1824 William Driver, a Salem sea captain, received a finely made flag from his friends and neighbors in the Massachusetts port. Delighted with the gift, Driver immediately hoisted it from his vessel, the *Charles Doggett,* exclaiming: "I name her 'Old Glory.' " The nickname soon won wide acceptance and has remained in use since that time. Captain Driver retired from the sea in 1837 and settled in Nashville, Tennessee. On patriotic days he proudly displayed Old Glory in front of his home. Tradition has it that he hid the flag between the folds of a comforter when Tennessee seceded from the Union in 1861 and then joyfully brought it out in February, 1862, as federal troops occupied the city. In 1922 the Driver family donated the flag to the Smithsonian Institution.

The year 1830 is notable in American history for its great war of words. Speaking in behalf of the nullification of federal laws were South Carolina's states' rights statesmen Robert Haynes and John Calhoun. Defending the national point of view were Massachusetts' Daniel Webster ("Liberty and union, now and forever, one and inseparable") and President Jackson ("Our Federal Union—it must be preserved"). Two years later the South Carolina legislature fitted action to words by calling a state convention. With little opposition this group declared "null, void, and no law" the 1828 and 1832 tariffs. This serious threat to national unity fizzled out suddenly when Congress passed two face-saving measures—a force bill empowering the President to enforce the tariff (in South Carolina) and then a compromise tariff that could and did make such action unnecessary. South Carolina's star remained in the national flag.

The Stars and Stripes received its first official recognition from the Army in 1834, fifty-seven years after its adoption. The *General Regulations* of that year marked the first attempt of the Army to prescribe some details of design. Article LV read: "The garrison flag is the national flag . . . to be composed of thirteen horizontal stripes of equal breadth, alternately red and white, beginning with the red. In the upper quarter, near the staff, will be the Union, composed of a number of white stars, equal to the number of States, distributed over a blue field, one-third the length of the flag, and to run down to the lower edge of the fourth red stripe from the top."

Article LV also authorized for the first time the carrying of the national flag by troops. "Each regiment of artillery shall have two silken colors. The first, or the national color, of stars and stripes, as described for the garrison flag. The number and name of the regiment to be embroidered with gold on the centre stripe . . ." The second, or regimental color, was to be two crossed cannon on a yellow field. (In 1886 the color of the field was changed to scarlet.) The infantry and cavalry (then called "dragoons") continued to carry their flags of blue. The infantry was also authorized a white regimental color announcing the unit designation.

On March 2, 1836, a new republic was born on the North American continent when Texas declared its independence from Mexico. The Texas legislature adopted two starred flags that year. For its naval ensign it took the design of the United States flag, substituting a large white star for the twenty-four stars then in the canton. For a national flag it chose a blue field bearing a large gold star in the center. In 1839 both of these banners were replaced by the famous Lone Star Flag that later became the Texas state emblem.

Meanwhile, under the flag of twenty-four stars, antislavery forces were building up such strength that they became an influential factor in Northern politics. Although small in number the abolitionists zealously carried their crusade into every free state and even into some places in the South. When Arkansas Territory adopted a state constitution in January, 1836, the anti-slavery element in Congress worked to block the admission of another slave state. It was pointed out that such action would give the Southerners a majority in the Senate. Finally a compromise was hammered out: Arkansas was to be admitted simultaneously with the new free state of Michigan. The entry of Michigan was stalled, however, by a local quarrel with Ohio over the Toledo strip. As a result, Arkansas entered the Union alone on June 15, 1836.

★ ★ ★ ★ ★ U.S.A. FLAG 1836–1837

Arkansas's star, the twenty-fifth, was added to the national flag July 4, 1836. Under this banner Democratic rule was extended another four years with the election and inauguration of Jackson's hand-picked successor, Martin Van Buren. Van Buren, born at Kinderhook, New York, in 1782, was the first President born under the flag of the United States.

The new President had barely moved into the White House when the nation was struck by its first severe depression of purely American origin. A rash of internal improvements had brought excessive extension of credits by banks and unwarranted borrowings by state governments. When New York City banks suspended specie payments May 10, 1837, the panic was on. Banks closed, businesses failed, and industry became paralyzed. For the next seven years economic depression hung over the land like a black fog.

Meanwhile Michigan's request for admission into the Union was stymied by the state convention's refusal to recognize Ohio's claim to the Toledo strip, even though offered the Upper Peninsula (from Wisconsin Territory) in exchange. Then, the local Democrats took over. In a "convention" that was no more than a party caucus they accepted Congress' terms for the entire state. Thus, Michigan, consenting only in part, was admitted into the Union January 26, 1837.

★　★　★　★　★　　U.S.A. FLAG 1837–1845

Under the flag of twenty-six stars (Michigan's star was added July 4, 1837) four Presidents occupied the White House. The first, Martin Van Buren, was a candidate to succeed himself in 1840. But he could not overcome two major political obstacles: (1) the hard times that had hit the nation; and (2) the rip-roaring, hard-cider and log-cabin campaign put on by the Whigs' "Tippecanoe and Tyler too." William Henry Harrison won in a landslide of electoral votes. After serving only one month Harrison died of pneumonia and John Tyler became the first vice-president to succeed to the office upon the death of a President. In 1844 the Whigs dumped Tyler as a candidate and chose Henry Clay. The Democrats nominated the first dark horse in history, James K. Polk, a Tennessee lawyer. A highly aggressive platform brought Polk victory—he pledged the "reannexation" of Texas and the "reoccupation" of Oregon ("Fifty-four forty or fight"). Polk was sworn in under this eighth Stars and Stripes, which became only the first of five different national flags in use during his single administration. Each Independence Day Polk was in office one additional star was added to the flag.

The Stars and Stripes of 1837–1845 served as the naval ensign of Lieutenant Charles Wilkes's historic exploring expedition into the waters of the Pacific and Antarctic oceans. During his four-year voyage, 1838–1842, Wilkes carried the national banner more than ninety thousand miles and proved that Antarctica was a continent.

In 1841, seven years after artillery had been authorized the use of the national flag, the infantry also received the right to carry the Stars and Stripes. The army *General Regulations* for 1841 (Article LII) provided that: "Each regiment of Infantry shall have two silken colors. The first, or the national color, of stars and stripes, as described for the garrison flag; the number and name of the regiment to be embroidered with silver on the centre stripe. . . ." The regimental standard was to be the old blue flag formerly carried as a national color. (This design became popular with many of the state legislatures. Almost half the state banners display the arms of the state on a blue field.) A white infantry color, authorized in 1834, was discarded.

During the 1840's when General John C. Frémont was earning his nickname as "Pathfinder of the West," he carried a Stars and Stripes as distinctive as his brilliant and erratic career. In the canton were the authorized twenty-six stars, arranged in two wavy lines of thirteen each. Between the two lines of stars was an eagle clutching in its talons a bundle of arrows and a calumet (ceremonial peace pipe). At that time a personalized Stars and Stripes was not illegal—merely distasteful. Frémont's flag is now preserved in the Southwest Museum, Los Angeles, California.

In the fall of 1842 occurred one of the Navy's greatest

embarrassments. Commodore Thomas Jones, hearing that the United States and Mexico were at war, sailed into Monterey Bay, hoisted the Stars and Stripes over the town, and proclaimed California a territory of the United States. Discovering his mistake the next day he hauled down the flag and withdrew with as much dignity as was possible under the circumstances.

Beginning in 1838 Florida earnestly sought entrance to the Union. It succeeded only when it became apparent that Iowa also was ready for statehood, and the two could then be paired off. In this way the balance between slave and free states would be retained. Florida gained admission March 3, 1845, but Iowa's entrance into the Union was postponed for another year and a half.

★ ★ ★ ★ ★ U.S.A. FLAG 1845–1846

On July 4, 1845, the twenty-seventh star (for Florida) was added to the national flag. Under this banner the United States was gripped by confusion, great excitement, and finally war. The focal point of national attention was Texas. For nine years the question of annexing this independent republic had caused a stormy controversy between the free and the slave states in the Union. Slavery was legal in Texas and the South hungered for additional strength in Congress. Many in the North thought annexation would touch off war with Mexico. Mexico itself had said quite emphatically that it would fight to prevent such action. Most Southerners were willing—even eager—to take that chance. Finally, on March 1, 1845, a lame-duck Congress and a lame-duck President (Tyler) had put their stamp of approval on annexation.

The same day Florida's star was added to the flag a Texas state convention accepted the statehood terms offered by the United States. The agreement was ratified by popular vote in October and on December 29 Texas entered the Union.

Too late to back down now, President Polk ordered General Zachary Taylor to move his camp from the Nueces River to the Rio Grande for the "protection of Texas." In April Mexican troops crossed the river and wiped out a United States cavalry detachment. Polk and his cabinet had been waiting for just such an incident. Mexico had "invaded our territory and shed American blood upon American soil." War was declared May 13, 1846.

In Texas, "Old Rough and Ready" Taylor had not been waiting for the formal declaration of war. On May 8–9 in the battles of Palo Alto and Resaca de la Palma he drove the Mexicans back across the Rio Grande, and then crossed the river himself a few days later. This was the first time in formal warfare that an official Stars and Stripes was carried in battle by the United States Army. Each regiment of artillery and of infantry carried the banner of twenty-seven stars.

The second front to be opened up was in California. Colonel Stephen Kearny readied the "Army of the West" to push across New Mexico to the Pacific. A second expedition, a peacetime exploring party headed by General Frémont, had crossed the Sierra Nevada into central California some months before. In March 1846, Frémont had fortified Gavilan (Hawk) Peak northeast of Monterrey and hoisted the American flag there. He withdrew to the north, however, when the Spanish commandant at Monterrey, General José Castro, showed signs of moving against the American outpost. Spurred on by Frémont and unaware of the declaration of war, a band of American settlers met at Sonoma on June 14 and proclaimed California an independent republic. For their national banner they raised the colorful Bear Flag. In the center of a white field was painted a picture of a grizzly bear. (Evidently the picture presented a less than accurate reproduction because the *Californios* derisively referred to it as a "hog.") The designer, William Todd, placed a red stripe across the bottom of the flag and a red star at the top near the hoist. Under the bear was the legend "California Republic." This flag later became the California state flag.

★ ★ ★ ★ ★   U.S.A. FLAG 1846–1847

The twenty-eighth star, for Texas, became a part of the national flag July 4, 1846. Because most of the nation's land and naval forces were already

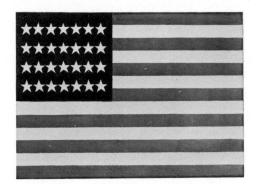

committed to action under the old banner with twenty-seven stars, the new Stars and Stripes did not come into widespread military use for some time.

While General Taylor was pushing the Mexican army back in the Southwest, President Polk's confidential agent, Thomas O. Larkin, was persuading the five hundred Americans in California to seek annexation to the United States. Commander John D. Sloat of the United States Navy added force to this argument. On July 7, 1846, he sailed into Monterey Bay and raised the American flag over the customhouse, claiming California for the United States. Two days later the short-lived California Republic came to an end when the Bear Flag was replaced by the Stars and Stripes at Sonoma. California was now an American territory, or rather, would be as soon as Colonel Kearny could march up from Santa Fe and force the final surrender. And that he did the following January.

In the meantime, General Taylor pressed his campaign in northeastern Mexico by occupying the towns of Monterrey, Saltillo, Victoria, and Buena Vista. This offensive was followed by the first large-scale amphibious operation in American history. On March 9, 1847, General Winfield Scott, with ten thousand men, landed at Vera Cruz on the Mexican east coast. After consolidating his position Scott launched a relentless drive into the interior, toward Mexico City.

Almost unnoticed in the excitement of war, Iowa was asking for admission as a state. Twice the Iowans rejected by popular vote Congressional attempts to provide them with a western boundary short of the Missouri River. Then finally Congress gave in and Iowa entered the Union December 26, 1846.

★ ★ ★ ★ ★   U.S.A. FLAG 1847–1848

The third and last official Stars and Stripes to fly during the Mexican War came into being July 4, 1847, when the twenty-ninth star was added for

Iowa. Because of the press of war it found competition in many places with national banners having but twenty-eight stars or sometimes twenty-seven. Even President Polk's White House staff must have had a difficult time insuring that the flags used at official functions bore the correct number of stars.

In Mexico, flying banners that were now outdated, Generals Taylor and Scott delivered the final knockout blows to Santa Anna's outgunned and outfought army. Scott took possession of Mexico City September 14, 1847, ending his seven-month drive westward from Vera Cruz. On February 2, 1848, Mexico signed the treaty of Guadalupe Hidalgo, accepting the Rio Grande boundary and ceding New Mexico and California to the United States in return for fifteen million dollars. At the conclusion of the war the Senate resolved unanimously "That the Vice-President be requested to have the flag of the United States first erected by the American army upon the palace in the capital of Mexico deposited for safekeeping in the Department of State of the United States." This flag had twenty-eight stars arranged in four even rows of seven each.

The balance between free and slave states was restored in 1848 when Wisconsin, the fifteenth free state, entered the Union. (With the admission of Iowa the previous year this offset the two-state majority obtained by the South when both Florida and Texas entered the Union in 1845.) In terms of boundary settlements Wisconsin had fared poorly during its status as a territory. In 1818 the Chicago area had been cut from its southern border to give Illinois a Great Lakes port.

Then in 1836 the Upper Peninsula had been awarded to Michigan to counterbalance that state's surrender of the Toledo strip to Ohio. The territorial government asked for internal improvements to offset these sizable losses. When this request was ignored, Wisconsinites pressed for statehood as the only means of protecting their interests. The state was admitted May 29, 1848, the fifth and last commonwealth carved out of the Northwest Territory.

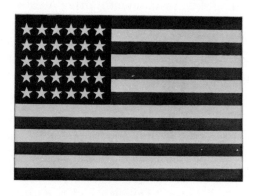

★ ★ ★ ★ ★   U.S.A. FLAG 1848–1851

The flag of thirty stars (Wisconsin's was added July 4, 1848) was the last Stars and Stripes to fly while Polk was President. It was also the flag of Zachary Taylor, the twelfth President, who died sixteen months after his inauguration in 1849, and the banner of Millard Fillmore who succeeded him. It was not the flag of a president named David R. Atchison. Atchison, a proslavery senator from Missouri, was president *pro tempore* of the Senate on March 4, 1849, when President-elect Taylor refused to take the oath of office because it was Sunday. Some historical thrill-seekers have therefore supposed that Atchison served as President of the United States for twenty-four hours. Actually, of course, Polk remained President until Taylor was sworn in at noon on March 5.

The Mexican War had provided the United States with vast new stretches of territory in the West. Out of it the Southerners hoped to carve new slave states. Their plan started to go awry, however, when the discovery of gold in California attracted some eighty thousand adventurers within a few months, most of these forty-niners migrating from the North and West. Consequently, when a convention at Monterey drafted a state constitution late in 1849, the document prohibited slavery. California was petitioning for admission as a free state! Enraged Southerners vowed secession if slavery were excluded from California. The North was almost as firm against any further extension of slavery.

When disunion seemed inevitable, Henry Clay offered his famous Compromise of 1850. For eight months Congress fought over Clay's proposals and then accepted them. The North agreed to (1) leave open the question of slavery in the new territories of New Mexico and Utah; and (2) give the South a stronger fugitive slave law. The South, in turn, agreed to (1) prohibit slave trade in the District of Columbia, and (2) admit California as a free state. California entered the Union September 9, 1850. Civil war was averted for another decade and the course of empire had run from the Atlantic to the Pacific.

★ ★ ★ ★ ★   U.S.A. FLAG 1851–1858

On July 4, 1851, the addition of California's star created a national flag of thirteen stripes and thirty-one stars. It was the flag of three Presidents—Millard Fillmore, the thirteenth; Franklin Pierce, who defeated the military hero of the Mexican War, Winfield Scott, in 1852; and James Buchanan, elected in 1856. Buchanan was to be the last Democrat elected to the nation's highest office for twenty-eight years. In the next Presidential election the new Republican party would win the first of six consecutive national administrations, a record unequaled in the history of modern American political parties. (Next longest record: the five straight victories won by the Democrats, 1932–1948.)

Abroad, the flag of thirty-one stars was the first American ensign to be displayed in Japan. On July 8, 1853, Commodore Matthew C. Perry sailed into Tokyo (Yedo) Bay under this banner and presented a letter from President Fillmore. Perry's flag is now in the Naval Academy Museum.

At home, the seven years under this flag might well be termed the era of the big build-up—a relentless building toward catastrophe. It was the era of *Uncle Tom's Cabin,* the underground railroad for fugitive slaves, bleeding Kansas, and the Dred Scott controversy. Most significant of all was the formation of a new political party, the Republican, dedicated to halt the expansion of slavery. Founded in 1854, the party nominated its first Presidential candidate, Frémont, two years later. Frémont ran a poor second to Buchanan. By 1858, however, the party had found a new spokesman, a craggy-faced, lanky lawyer from Illinois named Abraham Lincoln. On June 16 of that year Lincoln graphically analyzed the predicament of the nation: "A house divided against itself cannot stand. I believe this government cannot endure permanently half slave and half free."

The admission of California as a free state in 1850 severely handicapped the South's efforts to horse-trade over the admission of additional new states. The free states now had a definite majority in both houses of Congress. As a result, when Minnesota asked for entrance into the Union the Southern states could offer no more than token opposition. Minnesota was admitted May 11, 1858. The new federal-state governmental set-up marked the *fourteenth* and last political organization to function over all or part of the land of sky-tinted water. Earlier governments in order of their appearance had been: France, England, Spain, the colony of Virginia, the Northwest Territory, and the territories of Louisiana, Indiana, Illinois, Michigan, Missouri, Iowa, Wisconsin, and finally Minnesota.

★ ★ ★ ★ ★   U.S.A. FLAG 1858–1859

The flag of thirty-two stars came into being July 4, 1858, with the addition of a star for Minnesota. It was a time for strong words and firm action. But in all the land only one voice spoke with resolution and courage, that of Abraham Lincoln. And in the autumn Lincoln lost his bid for a seat in the Senate to the equivocating Stephen Douglas. Meanwhile, in the White House, President Buchanan weakly fumbled away any chance there was of preserving the peace. The end of an era had come. This was to be the last Stars and Stripes under which North and South could reconcile their differences short of war.

Out on the West coast, a slavery controversy within the territory itself retarded movement for Oregon's statehood. Finally, this issue as well as the new state constitution was submitted to the voters. Slaveholding was prohibited and the constitution ratified, both by large majorities. The largest vote, however, went in support of a measure prohibiting the admission of free Negroes into Oregon—the same restriction that had delayed Missouri's entry thirty years before. But there was no quibbling now and Oregon entered the Union February 14, 1859.

Musical note: On April 4, 1859, a song written by Daniel D. Emmett was sung for the first time, in New York. The song was "Dixie."

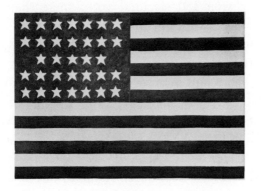

★ ★ ★ ★ ★ U.S.A. FLAG 1859–1861

On July 4, 1859, the thirty-third star, for Oregon, was added to the national flag. At that time thirty-three states acknowledged their federal unity under this ensign. Less than two years later, eleven of these states had repudiated their allegiance to the Stars and Stripes and had formed their own independent government, the Confederate States of America, under their own flag. The long-threatened breakup of the Union had come. The immediate cause was the Presidential election of 1860. Four major candidates were in the field, each with a different approach to the problem of slavery in the territories, the critical issue of the time. Abraham Lincoln (Republican) favored the prohibition of slavery expansion; Stephen Douglas (Northern Democrat) supported the doctrine of popular ("squatter") sovereignty; John Breckinridge (Southern Democrat) upheld unlimited expansion of slavery; John Bell (Constitutional Union) believed in further compromises. Although Lincoln received a minority of the popular votes, he won 180 electoral votes, more than double those of his nearest opponent, Breckinridge.

To the South, Lincoln represented the growing power of the federal government, a government that was becoming more and more dominated by free states. Five free states in a row had entered the Union since Texas, the last slave state, had been admitted in 1845. The struggle to bring Kansas into the Union as a slave state had been hopelessly lost. And now Lincoln was elected to head a "Black Republican" administration. This was too much. The South would leave the Union. South Carolina seceded first (December 20, 1860), then Mississippi, Florida, Alabama, Georgia, Louisiana, and Texas—all less than six weeks later.

While the slave states were leaving the Union, Kansas was preparing for admission. Created as a territory by the bitterly disputed Kansas-Nebraska Act of 1854, the new state was to be slave or free depending upon the decision of the Kansans themselves. This doctrine of squatter sovereignty had produced six years of internal war as proslavery and antislavery factions fought to dominate "Bloody Kansas." For a time the settlers from the South seemed victorious. A convention at Lecompton drew up a constitution legalizing slavery. Tested twice by popular vote, the constitution won a majority the first time, lost the second time. Nevertheless, in 1858 President Buchanan recommended that Congress admit Kansas as a slave state. The Senate voted to do so but the House balked, insisting that the Lecompton Constitution be resubmitted to popular vote. On the third try voters again rejected the document and the Southern cause was lost in Kansas. In 1859 a new constitution prohibiting slavery was framed at Wyandotte and ratified by popular vote, 10,421 to 5,530. Kansas entered the Union as a free state January 29, 1861.

CHAPTER 10

★ ★ ★ ★ ★

★ ★ ★ ★ ★

A HOUSE DIVIDED ▓▓▓▓▓

▓▓▓

"If any one attempts to haul down the American flag, shoot him on the spot." That was the telegraphic message sent out by President Buchanan's Secretary of the Treasury, John Adams Dix, on January 29, 1861. The order was wired to an unarmed treasury clerk in New Orleans, William H. Jones. When Louisiana seceded and state troops began seizing federal property, the conscientious Jones became worried about the fate of the *Robert McCelland,* a revenue cutter of the United States Treasury Department. Dix's wire, sent from Washington, D.C., in answer to Jones's request for instructions, never reached its destination. It fell into Confederate hands, as did the *Robert McCelland.* Even had the telegram been properly delivered it would have made no difference. Throughout the lower South, seceding states were taking over federal forts, arsenals, ships, and other governmental installations.

The one exception was Major Robert Anderson's command at Charleston. Anderson wisely withdrew his garrison from the indefensible Fort Moultrie to the more formidable Fort Sumter in the city's harbor. From here he defied Confederate demands to surrender.

As secession swept through the South various state and local banners were created to symbolize the "independence" movement. South Carolinians flew several different emblems, finally settling on a blue flag featuring a white palmetto and crescent. Louisiana hoisted a Pelican Flag and then changed its mind and adopted a banner of thirteen red, white, and blue stripes with a single yellow star on a red canton. Georgia, Virginia, and North Carolina displayed emblems much like their present state flags. Of all these rebellious banners none achieved the great sectional popularity of the Bonnie Blue Flag. This banner with its large white star on a blue field had once been the national flag of the short-lived Republic of West Florida (1810). In 1861 it was reintroduced and made famous by a little Irish comedian, Harry McCarthy, who stumped the Cotton Belt singing the stirring war song "The Bonnie Blue Flag." (When federal troops occupied New Orleans in 1862 General Benjamin ["The Beast"] Butler ordered a fine of twenty-five dollars for anyone caught singing, whistling, or playing the song.)

With secession a seemingly accomplished fact, the states of the lower South called a convention at Montgomery, Alabama, to organize a provisional government, the Confederate States of America. One of the earliest functions of the new government was to adopt an appropriate national flag. For that purpose a Committee on the Flag and Seal of the Confederacy was appointed with William P. Miles of South Carolina (later an aide to General Beauregard) as chairman. On March 4, 1861, the convention voted to accept the flag recommended by the committee: "The Flag of the Confederate States of America shall consist of a red field, with a white space extending horizontally through the centre, and equal in width to one-third the width of the flag; the red spaces above and below to be of the same width as the white. The union blue, extending down through the white space, and stopping at the lower red space; in the centre of the union, a circle of white stars, corresponding in number with the States of the Confederacy." The number of stars emblazoned on the "union" was seven. Credit for the design belongs to Nicola Marschall, a Prussian artist from Marion, Alabama, and later Louisville, Kentucky.

This flag, the famous Stars and Bars, was raised over the capitol at Montgomery the same day by Miss L. C. Tyler, granddaughter of ex-President John Tyler. Later the convention voted ninety dollars to Alexander B. Clitherall to pay for the making of this first official Confederate flag.

Miles, the flag committee chairman, had never approved the design voted by his group and five months later persuaded the convention to adopt a resolution: "That the Committee on the Flag and Seal be instructed to inquire into the expediency of so changing the Confederate flag as to make it more distinctive and more distinguished from the flag of the United States." But the provisional government had other troubles to worry about, and finally voted to pass such action to the "permanent" Congress that was to come into existence at Richmond the following year.

First Confederate flag at Harpers Ferry

In the meantime, all attention was directed toward the Stars and Stripes still flying over Fort Sumter. On April 6 the new President, Abraham Lincoln, notified South Carolina authorities that he was sending an expedition to provision the besieged garrison. Fearing a prolonged federal occupation, Confederate shore batteries opened fire on the fort six days later. After undergoing a bloodless bombardment of thirty-four hours Major Anderson hauled down the Stars and Stripes and surrendered. He and his men evacuated the fort April 14 after first running up the flag again and saluting it with fifty guns. (A Union soldier killed during the salute was buried on the premises.) The federal troops were then allowed to board United States Navy vessels anchored just outside the harbor.

This was open rebellion and Lincoln chose to regard it as such. He issued a call for seventy-five thousand volunteers, and more than that number of loyal militia responded. The South, now committed to force, put its own armies in the field. As tension built up, four more states withdrew from the Union in May and June and joined the Confederacy—Virginia, Arkansas, Tennessee, and North Carolina. Four other slave states, caught between two fires, remained officially loyal to the Union—Delaware, Kentucky, Maryland, and Missouri.

Within the Union itself, the national flag grew to thirty-four stars on July 4, 1861, when Kansas received recognition in the Stars and Stripes. But now the rising feeling of sectional hatred produced sentiment for removing one star for each state that had seceded. Some Union extremists made unauthorized flags with only twenty-three stars. Others decided to omit stars for the border states as well. And some even reduced the number of stripes to conform to their ideas of state loyalties.

The oddest proposal came from Samuel F. B. Morse, the noted inventor of the telegraph and then president of The American Society for the Promotion of National Union. Morse suggested that the Stars and Stripes be divided into two flags—the canton cut diagonally from top to bottom with twenty-three stars and the upper

six and a half stripes retained by the North; the eleven stars below the diagonal and the lower six and a half stripes to go to the South. Both flags would then be finished out in white to make the conventional rectangle.

All such proposals received a firm "No" from the President. Lincoln wanted no tinkering with the Stars and Stripes. This was not a war between two nations but an insurrection of eleven states against the lawful federal government. According to his view the seceding states still belonged in the Union and as a result the national flag should—and would—remain unchanged.

The national flag with thirty-four stars and the new Stars and Bars first served under fire July 21, 1861, along a little creek in northern Virginia called Bull Run. After a day-long engagement the Union Army began to fall back and then stampeded toward Washington. During the fighting, however, Southern soldiers learned an important fact about their Confederate banner: it would not do as a battle flag. It looked too much like the Stars and Stripes, particularly when hanging limp on a staff.

To remedy this confusion General Joseph E. Johnston, who at Bull Run shared the top Confederate command with General Pierre G. T. Beauregard, called for suggestions for a new flag. In his *Narrative of Military Operations,* Johnston described the event: "Many designs were offered, and of several presented, that by General Beauregard was selected. I modified it by making the shape square instead of oblong, and prescribed the different sizes for infantry (four by four feet), artillery (three by three feet), and cavalry (two and a half by two and a half feet)." (Two men claimed to have designed the model submitted by Beauregard—William P. Miles, and Edward C. Hancock of New Orleans who had given his original to Colonel J. B. Walton, commander of the Louisiana Washington artillery.)

This flag, with its blue saltier (or cross) on a red field, won immediate acclaim throughout the South. For decorative purposes a white border was sometimes added on the outer edges. The use of thirteen stars was more of an artistic than a political success. Kentucky and Missouri remained in the Union even though Southern sympathies ran strong in both states. Although the battle flag was not officially adopted, many Confederate soldiers never fought under any other banner.

For almost two years federal and Confederate forces fought their battles under these two flags—the Stars and Stripes (with thirty-four stars) and the Rebel Battle Flag, or Southern Cross, as it was often called. Probably the most famous flag story of the war concerned Barbara Frietchie, the ninety-seven-year-old Unionist of Frederick, Maryland. According to John Greenleaf

Whittier's poem, she defiantly waved the Stars and Stripes in the face of General Stonewall Jackson's men as they entered the city September 6, 1862.

> "Shoot, if you must, this old gray head,
> But spare your country's flag," she said.

And Jackson's stirring answer:

> "Who touches a hair of yon gray head
> Dies like a dog! March on!" he said.

This description of the incident by poet Whittier was based on third-hand information. Although Whittier later asserted that he believed the report, the accuracy of his imaginative informant is highly suspect. After the war, Mary A. Quantrill, also of Frederick, claimed that she was the one who displayed the Union flag during the Confederate occupation of the city. Regardless of the truth of either story Whittier's poem has made Barbara Frietchie an immortal American heroine.

In mid-1863 both sides altered their flags. For the South, the Congress at Richmond finally got around to designing a new flag. On May 1, 1863, it ordered "That the flag of the Confederate States shall be as follows: The field to be white, the length double the width of the flag; with the union (now used as a battle flag) to be a square two-thirds the width of the flag, having the ground red, thereon a broad saltier of blue bordered with white and emblazoned with white mullets, or five-pointed stars, corresponding in number to that of the Confederate States."

In the North, the national flag grew to thirty-five stars on July 4, 1863, when a star was added for the new state of West Virginia. Two years earlier the northwestern counties of Virginia had repudiated secession and organized their own Unionist government (with a constitution providing for gradual emancipation of slaves). The splinter state was recognized by the federal government and admitted to the Union June 20, 1863—the only state formed out of an existing one without the consent of the older commonwealth.

These two new banners received little recognition. Pressed by the demands of war, most Northern troops did not receive the flag with thirty-five stars and continued to carry the older banner. In the South, no new emblem could replace the Battle Flag in the affections of the soldier in butternut. Moreover, the newly adopted Confederate flag proved to be a dismal failure. Its unusual length (twice the hoist) gave it a misshapen appearance. And its large white field made it look too much like a flag of truce. For Confederate vessels, the

Secretary of the Navy ordered the Stars and Bars replaced by the new official flag but with the length reduced to a proportion of one and a half to one. Throughout the war the Southern navy used the Battle Flag in rectangular form as its jack. Like the army's usage this adoption was never officially confirmed.

In 1863, Vicksburg and Gettysburg. In 1864, Grant's drive on Richmond and Sherman's march through Georgia. Despite the most heroic resistance more and more battle flags were being captured by relentless Union pressure.

And the official Confederate banner, the unfortunately named "White Man's Flag"? The Richmond government hadn't forgotten its heraldic flop. On March 4, 1865, during its last days, the Confederate Congress tried to correct its ungainly ensign. It shortened the fly to conform to the size already in use by the Rebel navy and it added a wide vertical red bar at the outside edge. But now nobody cared. Least of all the outnumbered and ill-supplied Confederate soldier. To the last, regimental color-bearers carried their cherished saltiers, and it was these flags that General Robert E. Lee's troops surrendered at Appomattox Courthouse, April 9, 1865. The war was over.

Lincoln's "house divided" prophecy of seven years before had been realized. "I do expect it will cease to be divided. It will become all one thing, or all the other." And what it became was all free. Under the national flag of thirty-five stars secession and slavery were forever ended in the United States.

With a fine sense of the dramatic, Secretary of War Edwin M. Stanton ordered Robert Anderson to Charleston, South Carolina.

War Department, Adjutant-General's Office
Washington, March 27, 1865

General Orders, No. 50. *Ordered, first,* That at the hour of noon, on the 14th of April, 1865, Brevet Major-General Anderson will raise and plant upon the ruins of Fort Sumter, in Charleston harbor, the same United States flag that floated over the battlements of that fort during the rebel assault, and which was lowered and saluted by him and the small force of his command when the works were evacuated on the 14th of April, 1861 . . .

On the historic day the flag raising took place with "suitable ceremonies" including a hundred-gun salute. Unfortunately, the event commanded little public attention for only a few hours later Abraham Lincoln was shot as he sat in the President's box at Ford's Theater in Washington.

CHAPTER 11

★ ★ ★ ★ ★

★ ★ ★ ★ ★

FLAG OF A WORLD POWER

The United States emerged from the Civil War burdened by the heavy tasks of readjustment in the North and reconstruction in the South. For a time the nation made little progress. Then suddenly, about 1877, it began the spectacular growth that is still continuing today. Almost overnight the one-time rural republic became a giant industrial empire. At the same time it soared to international prominence and power, assuming ever-mounting responsibilities. By the middle of the twentieth century America had taken first rank among the free nations of the world.

Throughout this entire period the proud, sustaining symbol of the United States was its national flag, the Stars and Stripes. At the close of the Civil War it contained thirty-five stars. In less than fifty years, thirteen new stars were added to give representation to an equal number of new states. Then, when the roster seemed complete, other territories beyond the contiguous limits of the nation asked for statehood status, and the number of stars in the flag began to increase again.

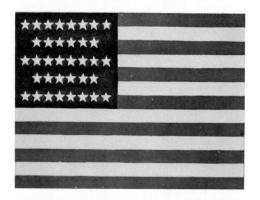

★ ★ ★ ★ ★ U.S.A. FLAG 1865–1867

The first postwar change in the flag was the addition of the thirty-sixth star, for Nevada, July 4, 1865. Created as a territory in 1861, Nevada was allowed to enter the Union on October 31, 1864, even though its population was only about twenty thousand, less than one-sixth of the number required for a single representative in the House at that time. Congress granted statehood so quickly because it wanted added support for ratification of the Thirteenth Amendment. The Sagebrush State did its part and the new amendment abolishing slavery went into effect December 18, 1865.

Under the flag of thirty-six stars Tennessee became

the first member of the late Confederacy to regain its full rights in the Union (July 24, 1866). The readmission of all the other seceded states was held up by a bitter fight between President Johnson and Congress over reconstruction policies. Meanwhile, far to the north, Alaska became United States soil on April 9, 1867, when the Senate voted to pay Russia $7,200,000 for "Seward's Folly."

When Nebraska sought entrance into the Union it provoked another clash between the executive and legislative branches of the national government. Like Nevada, the Cornhusker State had won statehood approval from Congress in 1864. But the Nebraskans were hesitant about entering the Union. (They had voted against it four years earlier.) Finally, in 1866 a state constitution was framed and ratified. At first Congress rejected the document because it enfranchised only white men. When the territorial legislature gave assurances that "white" meant any color whatsoever, Congress voted to admit Nebraska. President Johnson promptly vetoed the act, only to have it passed over his veto. At length Nebraska entered the Union on March 1, 1867.

★ ★ ★ ★ ★   U.S.A. FLAG 1867–1877

The thirty-seventh star, for Nebraska, was added to the national flag July 4, 1867. For the next ten years this Stars and Stripes waved over a nation struggling to throw off the painful effects of the Civil War—political, economic, social.

In politics it was a decade of complete Republican domination. The first President to serve under the flag

Flag of a World Power ★ 149

of thirty-seven stars was Andrew Johnson, a Tennessee Democrat who succeeded to office upon the death of Lincoln. But Johnson was powerless in the face of a runaway Republican Congress led by radicals who insisted on punishing the South. Three harsh reconstruction bills in a row were passed over the President's veto and in 1869 Johnson escaped conviction on impeachment by the narrow margin of one Senate vote. In the Presidential election that November, Republican candidate General Grant polled 214 out of 294 electoral votes. Grant's re-election in 1872 was notable as the first Presidential election in which every state chose its electors by popular vote. It was also unusual in that Grant's chief opponent, Horace Greeley, died before the Electoral College could meet after the election. As a result, his sixty-three electoral votes from six states were divided among four other candidates. Four years later the Presidential election became even more confused when double sets of electoral college returns were received from Florida, Louisiana, and South Carolina.

With nineteen electoral votes in dispute neither Republican Rutherford B. Hayes nor Democrat Samuel J. Tilden had enough votes to claim election. A special commission of fifteen members was then established to rule on the problem—five each of senators, representatives, and justices of the Supreme Court. Politically, eight were Republicans, seven Democrats. To no one's great surprise the commissioners voted to settle the dispute along strictly party lines, and Hayes was declared President, March 2, 1877, two days before inauguration time.

Meanwhile the once rebellious states were gradually readmitted as they complied with Congress' demands of political penance—six of them in 1868 over President Johnson's veto—Arkansas, North Carolina, South Carolina, Florida, Alabama, and Louisiana; and the four remaining sinners in 1870—Virginia, Mississippi, Texas, and Georgia (for the second time). Tennessee had rewon statehood rights in 1866. Thus, the third session of the forty-first Congress, convening in December 1870, was the first since 1860 in which every state was represented. Formal reconstruction finally ended April 24, 1877, when President Hayes withdrew federal troops from the last occupation outpost, New Orleans.

Another signpost of returning normalcy was the election of a Democratic House in 1874, the first in fifteen years. (At the next midterm election, in 1878, the Democrats captured control of both houses.) Contributing to the Republican slide was the financial panic of 1873 and the evil smell of corruption and scandal that pervaded Grant's second term.

On May 30, 1868, the flag of thirty-seven stars flew over the first observance of Decoration, or Memorial, Day—an expression of respect designated by the Grand Army of the Republic (Union veterans). Another note of national solidarity was sounded May 10, 1869, when the Atlantic-to-Pacific railroad connection was completed at Promontory Point, Utah. The whole country celebrated the driving of the final golden spike. And, finally, two new constitutional amendments became law—the fourteenth, giving the Negro civil rights (1868), and the fifteenth, granting him the right to vote (1870).

One hundred years after its founding the United States admitted its thirty-eighth state, Colorado, on August 1, 1876. In the century just closed twenty-five new states had entered the Union, almost double the original number. In terms of area and population, expansion was even more pronounced. According to the first federal census (1790), the flag of thirteen stars waved over an area of 892,135 square miles and 3,929,-214 people. Now the Stars and Stripes represented more than 3,000,000 square miles and more than 40,000,000 people.

Reflective military note: In May, 1871, United States naval vessels demolished five Korean forts in an effort to secure treaty relations with that nation. The task force finally retired without forcing an agreement from the Koreans. A more friendly approach secured a treaty of commerce and amity eleven years later.

★ ★ ★ ★ ★   U.S.A. FLAG 1877–1890

On July 4, 1877, Colorado's star, the thirty-eighth, was added to the national flag. The newest member of the Union thus became the Centennial State in a dual sense. Its admission the year before was on the hundredth anniversary of the Declaration of Independence and now its representation in the Stars and Stripes marked the centennial of the adoption of the national flag.

Five Presidents served under the flag of thirty-eight stars, equaling the number associated with the second Stars and Stripes (1795–1818). Rutherford B. Hayes finished his term in 1881 and was succeeded by another Republican, James Garfield. Four months after his inauguration Garfield was shot by a disappointed office seeker (Charles Guiteau) and died September 19. His vice-president, Chester A. Arthur, finished out the term. In a rough-and-tumble campaign in 1884 Grover Cleveland was elected, the first victorious Democratic nominee since Buchanan's triumph twenty-eight years earlier. Then four years later Cleveland was defeated by Benjamin Harrison, although the Democratic candidate received a clear plurality of the popular votes cast.[1]

Despite the relay race in the White House it was an unusually quiet thirteen years for the nation and its flag. The loudest noise came from the hammering of railroad spikes as 1880 introduced a period of unprecedented railroad construction—sixty-nine thousand miles of track laid in ten years. In 1882 Lieutenant Adolphus W. Greely, a Massachusetts soldier and explorer, carried the Stars and Stripes to within 497 miles of the North Pole (83°24′), the northernmost point yet attained. Unfortunately, two relief expeditions failed to reach Greely's party and sixteen of the twenty-three men in the group died of starvation on Cape Sabine before they could be rescued.

At home a financial crisis in 1884 caused almost eleven thousand banks to fail during the ensuing depression. Wage cuts provoked a wave of strikes and walkouts that reached a new nineteenth-century peak in 1886 with more than six hundred thousand workers out.

In June, 1887, President Cleveland enraged the Grand Army of the Republic by approving a War Department order for the return to the South of battle flags captured during the Civil War. After a week of angry protests by "bloody shirt" politicians and veter-

[1] Presidential elections are decided on the basis of a majority of the votes in the electoral college, not on the basis of total popular vote. In this election Cleveland won 5,540,329 popular votes, but carried only eighteen states with a total electoral vote of 168. Harrison, although receiving 100,000 fewer popular votes, carried twenty states having a total electoral vote of 233. Two other candidates gained the Presidency even though another man had a larger popular vote—John Quincy Adams and Rutherford B. Hayes.

Confederate Battle Flag (page 142)

Second Confederate Flag (page 143)

Third Confederate Flag (page 145)

Flag of Forty-Nine Stars (page 175)

ans, the President revoked the order on the grounds that such action was properly a function of Congress. In 1905, during the administration of Theodore Roosevelt, the flags were returned without protest.

When Cleveland was serving as a lame-duck President (his first term) he signed an omnibus statehood bill on February 22, 1889, providing for the admission of four states—North Dakota, South Dakota, Montana, and Washington. In November all four states were admitted —both Dakotas on the second, Montana on the eighth, and Washington three days later. Then just before the four stars were added to the flag, Idaho joined the omnibus states on July 3, 1890. The last recesses in the once-remote Oregon country were now filled in by full-fledged states.

★ ★ ★ ★ ★　　U.S.A. FLAG 1890–1891

The correct official flags that flew over the Independence Day celebrations in 1890 showed the addition of five new stars to the canton, the thirty-ninth through the forty-third. These honored five new states —North Dakota, South Dakota, Montana, Washington, and Idaho.

Unfortunately, few of the Stars and Stripes that flew that July 4—and on many of the succeeding days— showed the correct number of stars. When the four omnibus states entered the Union in November 1889, many flag makers prepared banners with forty-two stars in anticipation of the forthcoming July 4 change. But with the last-minute admission of Idaho on July 3 all such flags became unauthorized. Normally, a number of correct flags would have been manufactured, but just six days later (July 10) President Harrison signed a bill admitting Wyoming to the Union. Now, with the sure knowledge that all forty-three-starred flags would be obsolete in a year, few people bothered about displaying the correct Stars and Stripes. As a result a bewildering variety of national flags represented the United States for almost a year: some with forty-two stars; a few with the correct number of forty-three; others jumping the gun with forty-four stars; and, as usual, a host of unauthorized and obsolete banners with lesser numbers of stars.

Monetary note: The controversial fifty-first Congress (creator of the sky-high McKinley Tariff) adjourned in 1891 as the first "billion dollar" spending Congress in the nation's history.

Sports note: In 1891, at Springfield, Massachusetts, Dr. James Naismith invented basketball, the only major American sport with a purely American origin.

★ ★ ★ ★ ★   U.S.A. FLAG 1891–1896

The flag of forty-four stars came into being July 4, 1891, when Wyoming's star was added to the canton. At that time Benjamin Harrison was serving as the twenty-third President of the United States. When Harrison sought re-election the following year

he was defeated by Grover Cleveland, who had been the twenty-second President. The question then arose: Was Cleveland in his second term still the twenty-second President or was he now the twenty-fourth? Not a momentous problem, it is true, but one that persisted until 1950 when the *Congressional Directory*, the last major holdout, decided that Cleveland was really two Presidents, the twenty-second and twenty-fourth. Thus, in 1897 William McKinley became the twenty-fifth, and so on.

Under the flag of forty-four stars the nation's gigantic industrial expansion was suspended temporarily by another severe economic depression. A stock market crash on June 27, 1893, led to the failure of many banks and commercial houses, wage cuts, labor strife, and the typical business stagnation. One of the features of this depression was Jacob Coxey's army of unemployed, which marched from Massillon, Ohio, to Washington. Here it was spurned as a "nuisance" and its leader arrested for trespassing on the Capitol grass.

The last combat arm of the United States granted the right to carry the Stars and Stripes was the cavalry. The artillery and infantry had received such authorization before the Civil War, the engineers in 1866, and the Marine Corps ten years later. From 1863 to 1865 the cavalry had carried swallow-tailed guidons bearing the Stars and Stripes but this privilege was revoked by General Philip Sheridan after the war. In 1877 the War Department ordered cavalry regiments to carry a yellow standard charged with the national coat of arms. Then in 1895, at the instigation of the Quartermaster General, the Army ordered that for cavalry regiments "The national standard of stars and stripes, as described for flags, will be made of silk, 4 feet fly and 3 feet on the lance. . . ." The last important change in military flags as such came in 1904 when the regimental designation was removed from the national flag and placed on a silver band on the staff or pike.

On January 4, 1896, Utah was admitted to the Union, ending a long dispute between the federal government and the Mormon church over marriage laws. The Mormon ban of 1890 against polygamous marriage was now written into the new state constitution.

Holiday note: Labor Day, the first Monday in September, became a legal holiday by act of Congress on June 28, 1894.

★ ★ ★ ★ ★   U.S.A. FLAG 1896–1908

The forty-fifth star, for Utah, was added to the national flag July 4, 1896. Three Presidents served under this banner. President Cleveland's second term expired in 1897. He was followed by William McKinley, inaugurating fourteen years of unbroken Republican control of the Presidency and both houses of Congress. McKinley was re-elected in 1900 but was assassinated by an anarchist (Leon Czolgosz) the following year and succeeded by his vice-president, Theodore Roosevelt. The vigorous and popular Roosevelt won easily in 1904 over a Democratic party split by internal dissension. Meanwhile, the nation enjoyed a decade (1897–1907) of widespread prosperity.

In 1898 the United States began its thirty-third con-

secutive year of peace, the longest stretch in the nation's history without a major war. But at 9:40 P.M. of February 15 the quiet was suddenly shattered. In the harbor of Havana, Cuba, the battleship *Maine* exploded, killing two officers and 258 enlisted men. (When the *Maine's* hull was raised in 1911 examination showed that the cause of the explosion was external. The ensign that had been lowered at sunset on February 15 was recovered from its locker. The jack, found rolled up at the foot of the jackstaff ready for hoisting the following morning, was also recovered. Both flags are now preserved in the Naval Academy Museum at Annapolis.)

For three years Americans had worried about the great suffering in Cuba during that island's revolt against Spanish rule. This feeling, plus the cry "Remember the Maine," now produced a wave of anti-Spanish sentiment that was inflamed by the yellow journalism of many American newspapers. President McKinley tossed the ball to Congress and that body formally declared a state of war in existence as of April 21, 1898. The war ended 114 days later, with fighting generally restricted to Cuba, and to Manila Bay in the Philippines. At the peace table Spain freed Cuba and ceded Puerto Rico, the Philippines, and Guam to the United States. In return, the United States paid twenty million dollars to Spain for governmental buildings erected in these possessions.

The Stars and Stripes had now become the flag of a great imperial power with all the obligations and anxieties attendant upon such a position. Immediately, new problems popped up. These produced the first application of the "big stick," in Theodore Roosevelt's phrase, in Latin America, in the Philippines (during Aguinaldo's insurrection of 1899 to 1902), and in China (during the Boxer rebellion in 1900). Additional responsibilities were taken on in 1903 when the United States signed a treaty with the new Republic of Panama, obtaining the right to build a canal across the isthmus there.

Dramatic evidence of new-found power and prestige came in 1906 when President Roosevelt visited Panama and Puerto Rico aboard the battleship *Louisiana,* the first President to travel beyond the limits of national jurisdiction. There could be no more doubt about the ability of the United States to protect its citizens wherever the Stars and Stripes flew in the world. Further proof came 1907–1909 when a fleet of sixteen United States battleships carried the banner of forty-five stars around the world.

At home, Congress passed the first federal law concerning flag protocol on February 20, 1905. The act provided that no trademark could be registered if it "consists of or comprises the Flag or coat of arms or other insignia of the United States or any simulation thereof, or of any State or municipality or of any foreign nation. . . ."

Two years later in the celebrated case of *Halter* v. *Nebraska* the United States Supreme Court upheld the constitutionality of state statutes imposing penalties for desecration of the national flag. All the states in the Union now have specific laws prohibiting the desecration and other misuse of the Stars and Stripes. In sustaining such laws Supreme Court Justice John Marshall

Harlan of Kentucky called attention to the fact that the flag, which was "the emblem of freedom in its truest, best sense," was hardly intended for use on merchandise (in this case, a bottle of beer). The jurist said:

> A State will be wanting in care for the well-being of its people if it ignores the fact that they regard the Flag as a symbol of their country's power and prestige, and will be impatient if any open disrespect is shown towards it. By the statute in question the State has in substance declared that no one subject to its jurisdiction shall use the Flag for purposes of trade and traffic, a purpose wholly foreign to that for which it was provided by the Nation. Such a use tends to degrade and cheapen the Flag in the estimation of the people, as well as to defeat the object of maintaining it as an emblem of National power and National honor. And we cannot hold that any privilege of American citizenship or that any right of personal liberty is violated by a state enactment forbidding the Flag to be used as an advertisement on a bottle of beer. . . . As the statute in question evidently had its origin in a purpose to cultivate a feeling of patriotism among the people of Nebraska, we are unwilling to adjudge that in legislation for that purpose the State erred in duty or has infringed the constitutional right of any one. . . .

The United States admitted its forty-sixth state, Oklahoma, on November 16, 1907. Prior to 1889 this "Land of the Red People" (its Choctaw name) was unorganized Indian Territory, reserved exclusively for the settlement of Indians dispossessed elsewhere. Then on April 22, 1889, the western part was officially opened to land-hungry whites. Thousands poured into the region and a year later the Territory of Oklahoma was organized

164 ★ *Flags of the U.S.A.*

with a population of more than a quarter of a million. During the next few years the federal government opened up the remainder of the area by making individual land allotments to the Indians and buying up the "surplus" land in their reservations. In 1905 the Indians made one final bid for recognition. They organized their remaining lands into the state of Sequoyah and asked for admission into the Union. Congress refused, and in the following year passed an enabling act for all of present Oklahoma to be united into one state.

★　★　★　★　★　U.S.A. FLAG 1908–1912

On July 4, 1908, a new national flag came into being with the addition of the forty-sixth star for Oklahoma. Under this banner Theodore Roosevelt's term as President expired and his hand-picked successor, William Howard Taft, won election as the twenty-seventh President of the United States. The Republicans also maintained control of Congress but their long rule was drawing to a close. A party split between conservative "stalwarts" and progressive "insurgents" paved the way for a Democratic victory (the first since 1894) in the Congressional elections of 1910 and foretold the election of a Democratic President two years later.

The most heroic achievement under this flag took place in 1909 when cable and telegraph flashed to the world Admiral Robert E. Peary's proud message: "Stars and Stripes nailed to the North Pole." Peary had reached his goal April 6, thus ending three centuries of struggle to reach the most northern point on the globe.

In 1911 the nation prepared to welcome two new states, Arizona and New Mexico, which had long been territories. New Mexico Territory, which included all of present-day Arizona north of the Gila River, was established in 1850. The area south of the Gila was acquired in 1853 through the Gadsden Purchase of 45,535 square miles from Mexico. The purchase was arranged by the United States minister to Mexico, James Gadsden, grandson of the South Carolina Revolutionary hero Christopher Gadsden.

In 1863 Arizona became a separate territory. Settlement was slow, however, and it was not until 1910 that Congress passed a dual enabling resolution. This act was vetoed by President Taft because Arizona's constitution provided for the recall of judges. Finally, each state was admitted separately in 1912, New Mexico on January 6 and Arizona on February 14. All the territory within the contiguous borders of the United States was now embodied in forty-eight equal and sovereign states.

★ ★ ★ ★ ★   U.S.A. FLAG 1912–1959

The twenty-fifth Stars and Stripes to symbolize the United States of America came into being July 4, 1912, with the addition of the forty-seventh and forty-eighth stars for New Mexico and Arizona. It was to serve longer than any of its forerunners—forty-seven years. And it was the flag of a record number of Presidents—William H. Taft, 1912–1913; Woodrow Wilson, 1913–1921; Warren G. Harding, 1921–1923; Calvin Coolidge, 1923–1929; Herbert Hoover, 1929–1933; Franklin D. Roosevelt, 1933–1945; Harry S. Truman, 1945–1953; and Dwight D. Eisenhower, inaugurated 1953.

Of all these Presidents—as well as their twenty-six predecessors—the one who made the biggest contribution to the flag itself was William Howard Taft. Prior to 1912 the federal government had not established any official signs or proportions for the Stars and Stripes. As a result there was little uniformity in the appearance of the national flag. An administration survey showed

Flag of a World Power ★ 167

that government agencies alone were using national flags of sixty-six different sizes, most of them with varying proportions. The sizes and proportions of nongovernmental flags were even more chaotic. In the canton, most official flags, as well as most house flags, displayed the stars in a linear arrangement. But here too there was a wide variety of ingenious designs. A common practice was to arrange the stars in concentric circles, sometimes with a center star larger than the others.

In most government flags of forty-six stars the stars had been arranged in six rows, thus: 8–7–8–8–7–8. When it became certain that two more stars would be added for New Mexico and Arizona, the War and Navy departments established a joint board headed by Admiral George Dewey to recommend a common arrangement for the forty-eight stars. The board suggested six even rows of eight stars each. President Taft wisely approved the recommendation February 14, 1912. (The placing of the two new stars in the second and fifth rows disproved beyond question the popular belief that individual stars represented certain states according to the date of their admission into the Union.)

To establish some regularity in the form of the Stars and Stripes President Taft, by executive orders dated June 24 and October 29, 1912, limited "the sizes of flags manufactured or purchased for Government Departments" to those with the following hoists: 20 feet, 19 (standard), 14.35, 12.19, 10, 8.94, 5.14, 5, 3.52, 2.90, 2.37, and 1.31. The only exceptions were to be the flags carried by the armed services. The President also ordered these proportions for all national flags:

Hoist (height) of flag . . . 1 (unit)
Fly (length) of flag . . . 1.9
Hoist of canton . . . 7/13
Fly of canton . . . 0.76
Width of each stripe . . . 1/13
Diameter of each star . . . 0.0616

Accompanying the executive order was a plan furnished by the Navy Department showing the exact configuration of the national flag. On May 29, 1916, this executive order was revoked by President Wilson and new regulations issued. The basic provisions of the 1912 order were retained, however. President Wilson disapproved only the United States Navy practice of flying flags with only thirteen stars on small boats. He also altered the flag of the President (which was again redesigned by President Truman in 1945).

The exact shades of color to be used in the national flag were standardized for the first time in 1934. These are described by number in the Federal Standard Stock Catalog.

Under the flag of forty-eight stars the United States played an ever larger role in international affairs. In 1917 it threw its industrial and military might on the Allied side to force Germany's surrender in World War I. Then came two decades of peace—the roaring twenties and the depression-racked thirties. In 1941, two years after the outbreak, in Europe, of World War II, the United States again plunged into a global conflict, fighting two major wars simultaneously—one in the Pacific against imperial Japan, the other in Africa and

United Nations flag

Europe against the totalitarian might of Germany and Italy. Even before the war was concluded the United States helped create and then joined the United Nations, an international organization dedicated to preserving peace in the world. But peace proved more elusive than ever. A cold war split the world into two armed camps, Communist and Allied. While the major powers eyed each other suspiciously, fighting erupted in Korea. From 1950 to 1953 American troops fought in Korea to halt a Communist invasion of that divided country. And here for the first time soldiers, sailors, and airmen fought under an international flag—the blue and white banner of the United Nations—as well as under the Stars and Stripes.

Turbulent years of peace and war with many great accomplishments under the flag of forty-eight stars. A population surge from ninety-four to more than one hundred and seventy million. Creation of the North Atlantic Treaty Organization, the United States' first peacetime military alliance with nations outside the Western Hemisphere. The harnessing of atomic energy. All-time highs in production, employment, and the

Flag raising at Iwo Jima (1945)

standard of living. And seven amendments to the Constitution—sixteenth (1913) authorizing federal income taxes; the seventeenth (1913) providing popular election of senators; the eighteenth (1920) establishing prohibition; the nineteenth (1920) granting suffrage to women; the twentieth (1933) eliminating lame-duck Presidents and Congresses; the twenty-first (1933) repealing prohibition; and the twenty-second (1951) limiting the President to two terms, or to ten years, in office.

Turbulent years of war and peace. And countless heroic deeds under forty-eight starred flags that will be cherished as long as the nation lives. Some of these proud banners have not yet been enshrined to take their place with the historic representatives of earlier national flags but the list is already impressive. At the Marine Corps Museum in Quantico, Virginia, is the famous Stars and Stripes that was raised on Mount Suribachi during the bloody struggle for Iwo Jima in 1945. At the United States Military Academy at West Point is a fragment from the Stars and Stripes that was hidden when Corregidor fell in 1942, the flag that waved defiance over encircled Bastogne in 1944, and the flag that flew over SHAEF (Supreme Headquarters, Allied Expeditionary Force) during the Allied invasion of Germany 1944–1945.

Russian-American Company (1799-1861) (page 176)

Russian Ensign (1861-1867) (page 176)

Alaska State Flag (page 179)

Hawaii State Flag (page 186)

★ ★ ★ ★ ★

★ ★ ★ ★ ★

CHAPTER 12

THE FORTY-NINTH ▓

STAR IN THE FLAG ▓

The forty-ninth star, for Alaska, created the twenty-sixth Stars and Stripes and made obsolete the flag of forty-eight stars flown since 1912.

Alaska's entrance into the union produced several newsworthy items. (1) The new state's area of 586,400 square miles made it the largest in the nation, more than double that of Texas, which is second in size. (2) For the first time in history the Union had been extended to include a state that lies outside the contiguous boundaries of the United States. (3) Alaska represents the only state carved out of territory that was purchased by the United States from Russia.

The winning of statehood status came ninety-one years after the territory had come under the United States flag. Previously Russia had claimed Alaska on the basis of landings made along the coast by Vitus Bering and Alexei Chirikov in 1741. During the half century that followed, a profitable fur trade attracted hardy adventurers from Russia, Spain, England, France, Canada, and the United States. In 1799 the Russian government organized a semiofficial corporation, called the Russian-American Company, to regulate the fur trade and other commercial enterprises in the area. Chartered for twenty years, the Russian-American Company twice received twenty-year renewals. In 1861, however, the administration of Alaskan affairs reverted to the Czarist government.

There was some American interest in buying Alaska during the administration of President Buchanan. The Russian government seemed willing to sell, but the Civil War in the United States postponed official negotiations. Finally on March 30, 1867, President Johnson's Secretary of State, William H. Seward, completed the purchase for $7,200,000, or about two cents an acre. In a formal ceremony at Sitka on October 18 that year, the Russian flag was lowered and the United States flag became the official emblem of the territory formerly called Russian America. The ceremonial flag carried thirty-six stars although another star, for Nebraska, had been added July 4 that year. The historic emblem is now preserved in the Alaska Historical Library and Museum at Juneau.

The population of Alaska at that time was about thirty thousand. Many Americans thought so little of the seemingly remote wilderness territory that they called it "Seward's Folly" or "Seward's Ice Box." For a long time progress was slow and the criticism appeared justified. Even the federal government took little interest in the new acquisition. It did not provide Alaska with civil government until 1884.

Alaska's first boom came in 1896 with the discovery of gold in the Klondike region of Canada. The Alaska Panhandle provided the most accessible route to the gold fields, and prospectors swarmed through Skagway and the treacherous Chilkoot Pass. Three years later a new gold strike near Nome brought in thousands of new immigrants. In 1902 a third gold rush centered in the Fairbanks area. This was a violent, colorful era, made known to millions by the stories of Jack London and Rex Beach, and the poems of Robert W. Service.

Meanwhile the Klondike gold rush had pointed up the importance of the water inlets in the Alaska Panhandle. Both Great Britain (speaking for Canada) and the United States claimed ownership. The British position was that the boundary line between Alaska and Canada followed the outer edges of the promontories; the United States said that the line followed the heads of the bays and inlets. In 1904 the United States and Great Britain agreed to arbitrate the dispute before a six-man commission (three British and three Americans). By a four-to-two vote the commission upheld the United States claim.

Alaska won the right to send an elected delegate to Washington, D.C., in 1906. Six years later it achieved home rule with the granting of territorial status. At that time the population was about 60,000. By 1940 the number of Alaskans had grown to only 72,524.

A new era of rapid development opened with the

coming of World War II and the air age. The future forty-ninth state zoomed into world-wide importance as a defensive outpost of the United States, and it is now the site of valuable bases for the United States Army, Navy, and Air Force. Alaska is also a vital avenue of air travel as it lies across the most direct route from mid-America to eastern Siberia, Tokyo, and Manila. In addition to air lines and steamship routes. the northern-most state is connected to the rest of the Union by the Alaska Highway, completed during World War II. As evidence of its new boom the population increased by more than 75 per cent between 1940 and 1950, to 128,643. It continued to grow so rapidly that at the time of statehood the figure was estimated at more than 200,000.

Alaska took a long step toward statehood in 1946 when it conducted a territory-wide referendum on the subject. By a three-to-two ratio, voters approved the plan to become a state. The first Congressional hearings took place in 1947 and 1948 but the bill to admit the new state did not reach a vote. For the next ten years Congress debated the admission of Alaska, but each session adjourned without taking any action. The last near miss came in 1954 when the House of Representatives voted a bill calling for the admission of Hawaii as the forty-ninth state. Instead of accepting the House bill, the Senate voted to admit both Hawaii and Alaska as states. This measure died in the House.

Finally on June 30, 1958, both houses of the eighty-fifth Congress, in its second session, passed a bill admitting Alaska as a state. President Eisenhower signed the measure into law. The bill specified that before the new state could be admitted to the Union, the voters of Alaska must approve by referendum three separate propositions. Alaskans were asked to vote on (1) immediate statehood; (2) the state boundaries as outlined in the bill (similar to the territorial boundaries); and (3) all other provisions of the bill, the most important authorizing federal control over some public lands.

On July 16 the territorial governor, Mike Stepovich, set the referendum for August 26. On that date voters approved all three propositions by five-to-one margins. At the same time the new state held its first primary election, nominating candidates for its two seats in the Senate and one in the House. The first general election was held November 25.

Alaska's entry into the Union added a forty-ninth flag to the colorful array of banners representing the various states. The new state emblem had its beginning in 1927 during the administration of Alaska Governor George A. Parks. In that year the Alaska Department of the American Legion held a flag contest to find a suitable design for a territorial flag. The contest, open to all Alaskan school children enrolled in grades seven through twelve, attracted 142 designs. The winning award was submitted by thirteen-year-old Benny Benson, a seventh-grade pupil in the Territorial school at Seward, and resident of the Jesse Lee Mission Home. His design consisted of eight gold stars on a blue flag, with these words written below:

> The blue field is for the Alaska sky and the forget-me-not, an Alaskan flower.

The North Star is for the future state of Alaska, the most northerly of the Union.

The dipper is for the Great Bear—symbolizing strength.

In May 1927 the Territorial legislature incorporated young Benson's design into the official flag of Alaska. The act stated:

> . . . that the design of the official flag is eight gold stars in a field of blue, so selected for its simplicity, its originality and its symbolism. The blue, one of our national colors, typifies the evening sky, the blue of the sea and of mountain lakes, and of wild flowers that grow in Alaskan soil, the gold being significant of the wealth that lies hidden in Alaska's hills and streams.
>
> The stars, seven of which form the constellation Ursa Major, the Great Bear, the most conspicuous constellation in the Northern sky, contains the stars which form the "Dipper," including the "Pointers" which point toward the eighth star in the flag, Polaris, the North Star, the ever constant star for the mariner, the explorer, hunter, trapper, prospector, woodsman, and the surveyor. For Alaska the Northernmost star in the galaxy of stars and which at some future time will take its place as the Forty-ninth star in our National Emblem.

The legislature also appropriated a thousand dollars to send Benny Benson to Washington, D.C., to present the first flag to President Coolidge. When the trip failed to materialize, the legislature appropriated the money for the boy's education after leaving the Territorial school. The first flag, as well as all the designs submitted in the contest, are preserved in the Alaska Historical Library and Museum.

To acquaint the school children of Alaska with their

flag, the Territorial Commissioner of Education sent each student a small flag together with a poem written by Marie Drake, Deputy Commissioner.

Alaska's Flag

Eight stars of gold on a field of blue—
Alaska's flag. May it mean to you
The blue of the sea, the evening sky,
The mountain lakes, and the flow'rs nearby;
The gold of the early sourdough's dreams,
The precious gold of the hills and streams;
The brilliant stars in the northern sky,
The "Bear"—the "Dipper"—and, shining high,
The great North Star with its steady light,
Over land and sea a beacon bright.
Alaska's flag—to Alaskans dear,
The simple flag of a last frontier.

A musical score for the poem was written by Mrs. Eleanor Dusenbury, wife of the commanding officer at Fort William Seward. Published in 1940, the song "Alaska's Flag" is now sung in the schools of the forty-ninth state.

★ ★ ★ ★ ★

★ ★ ★ ★ ★

CHAPTER 13

HAWAII ADDS THE

FIFTIETH STAR

The fiftieth star, for Hawaii, was added to the national flag July 4, 1960. This addition created the twenty-seventh Stars and Stripes and rendered obsolete the one-year flag of forty-nine stars.

The admission of Hawaii into the Union climaxed more than a half century of effort to win statehood status for this group of islands. The first formal request came in 1903. It was rejected. In 1937, a Congressional committee investigated the possibility of admitting Hawaii as a state. It reported adversely, giving as reasons the mixed character of the population and the detached position of the island group. Later several statehood bills won approval in the House of Representatives only to be blocked in the Senate by political expediency and prejudice. In all, more than a dozen unsuccessful attempts were made to bring the territory into the Union as a state.

In 1950 a Hawaiian convention drew up a state constitution which was ratified later that year by popular vote, 82,788 to 27,109. When Alaska won Congressional approval for statehood in 1958, Hawaii gained new hope for admission into the Union. This hope was finally realized the following year when both houses of Congress voted to admit Hawaii as the fiftieth state. President Eisenhower signed the measure into law six days later, on March 18, 1959.

In a special election held June 27, 1959, Hawaii voted overwhelmingly "yes" to three statehood propositions:

1. Shall Hawaii immediately be admitted into the Union as a state?
2. Does Hawaii consent to the exclusion of Palmyra Island from the boundaries of the new state?
3. Does Hawaii accept statehood under all other conditions specified in the statehood bill, including land grants and reservations and one member of the House of Representatives?

On the same date the new state held its first primary election, nominating candidates for governor, lieutenant governor, the state legislature, two United States Senate seats, and one House seat. The victorious candidates won their offices in a general election held July 28. Three weeks later President Eisenhower officially proclaimed Hawaii a state and announced the design of the new flag of fifty stars.

The Hawaiian Islands were discovered by Captain

James Cook, the famous English navigator, in 1778. Cook named the group the Sandwich Islands in honor of his patron, the fourth Earl of Sandwich (more famous as the man who supposedly invented the "sandwich" as a quick snack when he was too busy gambling to eat a regular meal). Early visitors called the "big island" Owhyhee, an approximation in English spelling of the native name. After missionaries had reduced the Hawaiian language to written form the more correct spelling, Hawaii, was used. Today the name is usually applied to the whole group, especially by mainlanders.

By 1795 Kamehameha, the chief of the largest island, had united all the islands into one kingdom (except Kauai, which was added later). Kamehameha and his descendants reigned for almost a century. In 1850 Kamehameha III founded the city of Honolulu and made it the capital of the kingdom. He also gave the islands their national motto—"*Ua mau ke ea o ka aina i ka pono*" ("The life of the land is perpetuated by righteousness"). It was this king, too, who first proposed incorporating Hawaii into the United States.

During President Arthur's administration Hawaii was declared to be included under the protection of the Monroe Doctrine. Six years later (1887) the United States obtained exclusive right to establish a naval coaling and repair station on the Pearl River on Oahu Island.

The Hawaiian monarchy ended in 1893 when Queen Liliuokalani was deposed by a political revolution led by a "Committee of Safety," and supported by the

American minister John L. Stevens. Stevens then proclaimed Hawaii to be a United States protectorate and raised the Stars and Stripes over government buildings in Honolulu. Sanford B. Dole became president of the new government. A treaty of annexation was framed and submitted to the United States Senate. Before the Senate could act, Grover Cleveland replaced Benjamin Harrison in the White House and the new President immediately withdrew the treaty from consideration. He charged that the prominent part played by Americans in the revolution was "shocking." The Republic of Hawaii was founded the following year and won recognition from the United States August 7, 1894. Another annexation treaty was prepared in 1897 during President McKinley's administration but Senate ratification was stalled by the opposition of Democrats and anti-imperial Republicans. Additional opposition came from ex-Queen Liliuokalani, who was then in Washington, and from the Japanese government, which was worried about the status of its 25,000 nationals in Hawaii.

The Spanish-American War of 1898 dramatized the strategic value of Hawaii as a naval base and brought increased demand for annexation. To circumvent the two-thirds vote required for treaty ratification in the Senate, annexation was proposed in the form of a joint Congressional resolution requiring only a simple majority in both houses. By this method the annexation treaty was adopted by Congress and signed into law by President McKinley July 7, 1898. The official transfer took place August 12. Two years later, the islands were accorded full territorial status, June 14, 1900, with Sanford Dole as the first governor.

A little more than two thousand nautical miles from San Francisco, Hawaii has a total area of about 6,400 square miles and a population of about 600,000. Among the states in the Union it ranks forty-seventh in area—followed by Connecticut, Delaware, and Rhode Island—and forty-fifth in population—exceeding Vermont, Delaware, Wyoming, Nevada, and Alaska. Its largest islands are eight in number—Hawaii, Maui, Oahu, Kauai, Molokai, Lanai, Niihau, and Kahoolawe. Its two largest cities are Honolulu and Hilo.

The Hawaiian territorial flag showed the influence of the British Union flag, which the English explorer Captain George Vancouver presented to King Kamehameha I during the 1790's. The king was so pleased with his new possession he had it flown over the royal residence. In 1845 the Hawaiian legislative council established a new banner which was adopted by the territorial government of Hawaii in 1925. In the canton is the British Union device of three combined crosses—those of St. George, St. Andrew, and St. Patrick. The eight stripes of white, red, and blue in the field represent the eight main islands of the Hawaiian group. Article XIII, sec. 3, of the state constitution states: "The Hawaiian flag shall be the flag of the State."

★ ★ ★ ★ ★

★ ★ ★ ★ ★

CHAPTER 14

FLAG DAY AND FLAG

PLEDGE

The first nationwide observance of June 14 as Flag Day came in 1877 on the hundredth anniversary of the original flag resolution. The emphasis, however, was on the centennial rather than on the day itself. Twelve years later, George Bolch, principal of a free kindergarten for the poor in New York City, held some patriotic exercises on June 14. The ceremony attracted the attention of the New York legislature, which passed a law providing that: "It shall be the duty of the State Superintendent of Public Schools to prepare a program making special provision for observance in the public schools of Lincoln's Birthday, Washington's Birthday, Memorial Day, and Flag Day." The state superintendent then ordered that the flag be displayed on these days beginning at nine o'clock in the morning and that proper patriotic ceremonies be carried out.

During the remainder of the 1800's there was intermittent agitation for the recognition of June 14 as Flag Day. In 1893 the mayor of Philadelphia ordered the hoisting of the Stars and Stripes on public buildings on that day. This action was in response to a resolution passed by the society of Colonial Dames of Pennsylvania, then headed by Elizabeth Duane Gillespie, a descendant of Benjamin Franklin. The resolution also asked that June 14 be known as Flag Day and that private citizens take part in displaying the flag in their homes and places of business. Four years later (1897) the governor of New York proclaimed that the national flag should be displayed on all public buildings on June 14.

Meanwhile, the American Flag-Day Association was formed at Chicago in 1894 to promote the formal recognition of the third Saturday in June as Flag Day. Two years later the group decided that June 14 was a more appropriate day. Bernard J. Cigrand, a United States Navy officer and flag historian, took a leading part in placing the emphasis on June 14. But the idea caught on very slowly. The first state to establish the June 14 Flag Day as a legal holiday was Pennsylvania, on May 7, 1937.

Winning national recognition took even longer. President Wilson in 1916 and President Coolidge in 1927 issued proclamations asking that June 14 be observed as national Flag Day. But it was not until August 3, 1949, that Congress finally gave its approval to the project. In a joint resolution it resolved: "That the 14th day of June of each year is hereby designated as Flag

Day and the President of the United States is authorized and requested to issue annually a proclamation calling upon officials of the Government to display the flag of the United States on all Government buildings on such day, and urging the people to observe the day as the anniversary of the adoption on June 14, 1777, by the Continental Congress of the Stars and Stripes as the official flag of the United States of America." President Truman signed the measure into law the same day.

★ ★ ★ ★ ★ THE PLEDGE OF ALLEGIANCE CONTROVERSY

"I pledge allegiance to the flag of the United States of America and to the Republic for which it stands, one Nation under God, indivisible, with liberty and justice for all."

The authorship of this pledge has been disputed almost as much as the origin of the flag itself. The story begins in Boston in the offices of *The Youth's Companion,* a publication with a large circulation among the girls and boys of America. James B. Upham, head of the circulation department, was determined to promote a revival of "old-fashioned" patriotism, which seemed to be going out of style about 1890. There was, for example, a sneering editorial in the Boston *Herald* which referred to flag raisings as "the worship of a textile fabric." Upham's plan was to stimulate love of flag and country by encouraging children to buy their own flag for display over schoolhouses. The program worked amazingly well and within a year the Stars and Stripes had been raised over an estimated thirty thousand schools from Maine to California. The climax of the program was to come in 1892 on the four hundredth anniversary of Columbus Day. Due in large part to the untiring efforts of Upham and a young associate, Francis Bellamy, Congress passed a joint resolution authorizing President Harrison to declare October 12 a legal holiday with celebrations centered in the schools.

One final task remained. Upham wanted to provide some kind of vow to be recited aloud when the flag was raised. Many schools were employing the pledge "I give my hand and heart to my country, one nation, one language, one flag." Upham thought this unsatisfactory. He wanted, "in few words, a sentiment as big as the day itself. It must be so fundamental, and so stirring, that it will live if possible long after this one occasion."

Upham tried to write a new and more impressive pledge of allegiance. His co-worker, Francis Bellamy, also tried his hand at creating just the right phraseology. Finally, in August, 1892, a new formula was composed:

"I pledge allegiance to my flag and to the Republic for which it stands—one Nation indivisible, with liberty and justice for all." The new pledge, first recited the following Columbus Day, was an immediate success.

Some years later, after the pledge had become a national institution, the identity of the author was asked. It is at this point that the story becomes controversial. The members of Upham's family claimed that he was the author. Others denied this and said that Francis Bellamy wrote the enduring words. The question provoked debate for years. Eventually, the United States

190 ★ *Flags of the U.S.A.*

Flag Association (an organization now defunct) appointed a committee to determine just who the author was. The committee (three university professors) heard all the evidence and on May 18, 1939, reached a unanimous verdict. The honor belonged to Bellamy. Despite this decision others remain convinced that James B. Upham was the sole author. Most of the support for Upham came from the United States Flag Foundation, a patriotic organization formed to promote proper respect for the flag.

Actually, the whole controversy is pointless. The authorship must be regarded as a joint effort, for Upham and Bellamy discussed the proposed pledge many times and at great length. Bellamy himself, after stating that he wrote the final draft, admitted that "the occasion for it was in the large soul of that rare and self-retiring patriot, James B. Upham."

At the National Flag Conferences of 1923 and 1924 delegates from patriotic societies and civic and other organizations made one change in the wording of the pledge. The phrase "flag of the United States of America" was substituted for "my flag" so that the meaning would be unmistakable. This was the form adopted by Congress in 1942 when the pledge of allegiance was incorporated into the national flag code. The phrase "under God" was added by Congress on June 14, 1954.

When Congress approved the pledge in 1942 it also sanctioned considerable latitude in the so-called flag salute, given as the pledge is being recited. Section 7 of the flag code states that the proper salute is: ". . .

standing with the right hand over the heart. However, civilians will always show full respect to the flag when the pledge is given by merely standing at attention, men removing the headdress. Persons in uniform shall render the military salute." Before this time, several different types of salute had been used—the right arm extended toward the flag, palm up; the right hand over the heart; and the military salute by civilians. Some states passed laws requiring a certain type of salute. This action was protested by some minority groups and eventually the courts ruled on a Pennsylvania law requiring school children to render a hand salute to the flag. In Minersville, Lillian Gobitis, age twelve, and her brother William, age ten, refused to salute the flag and were expelled from school. Their parents, members of the Jehovah's Witnesses sect, obtained an injunction from a local court forbidding school authorities to make the flag salute compulsory. A higher Pennsylvania court sustained the lower court, but the United States Supreme Court threw out the injunction, ruling that it was legal for a state to require a formal salute to the flag.

This decision stood for only three years. In 1943 the Supreme Court reversed itself when the test of a similar state law reopened the question (*West Virginia State Board of Education* v. *Barnette*). At that time the Court invalidated such laws as infringing the First Amendment, a decision that still stands.

CHAPTER 15

★ ★ ★ ★ ★

★ ★ ★ ★ ★

FLAG CODE AND

TRADITION

Ever since its adoption in 1777 the Stars and Stripes has earned and received the respect of all Americans. During its long history many customs and traditions have developed regarding the proper display and usage of the flag. The armed forces have issued their own regulations to insure uniform respect for the flag. For many years, however, civilians had no formal rules to follow in matters of flag etiquette. In 1923 representatives from business, patriotic, and civic groups held a National Flag conference in Washington, D.C. This conference, and a second one held the following year, drew up a national code prescribing the correct manner of displaying and respecting the flag of the United States.

In 1942, by joint resolution, Congress adopted this code as federal law. It was approved by President Franklin D. Roosevelt on December 22, 1942. With the exception of minor changes this is the same federal flag code that is in effect today. These are the changes:

(1) Section 2(d): November 11, formerly called Armistice Day, is now known as Veteran's Day; (2) Section 3(c): rules governing the display of the Stars and Stripes with the United Nations flag were added by Congress in 1953; and (3) Section 7: the part dealing with the pledge of allegiance was reworded in 1945 and amended in 1954 to add the words "under God" to the pledge.

The present code in its entirety is as follows:

Resolved by the Senate and House of Representatives of the United States of America in Congress Assembled, That Public Law Numbered 623, approved June 22, 1942, entitled "Joint resolution to codify and emphasize existing rules and customs pertaining to the display and use of the flag of the United States of America," be, and the same is hereby amended to read as follows:

That the following codification of existing rules and customs pertaining to the display and use of the flag of the United States of America be, and it is hereby, established for the use of such civilians or civilian groups or organizations as may not be required to conform with regulations promulgated by one or more executive departments of the Government of the United States.

★ ★ ★ ★ ★ DISPLAY, HOISTING, AND
LOWERING

Sec. 2 (a) It is the universal custom to display the flag only from sunrise to sunset on buildings and on stationary flagstaffs in the open. However, the flag may be displayed at night upon special occasions when it is desired to produce a patriotic effect.

(b) The flag should be hoisted briskly and lowered ceremoniously.

(c) The flag should not be displayed on days when the weather is inclement.

(d) The flag should be displayed on all days when the weather permits, especially on New Year's Day, January 1; Inauguration Day, January 20; Lincoln's Birthday, February 12; Washington's Birthday, February 22; Army Day, April 6; Easter Sunday (variable); Mother's Day, second Sunday in May; Memorial Day (half staff until noon), May 30; Flag Day, June 14; Independence Day, July 4; Labor Day, first Monday in September; Constitution Day, September 17; Columbus Day, October 12; Navy Day, October 27; Veterans' Day, November 11; Thanksgiving Day, fourth Thursday in November; Christmas Day, December 25; such other days as may be proclaimed by the President of the United States; the birthdays of States (dates of admission); and on State holidays.

(e) The flag should be displayed daily, weather permitting, on or near the main administration building of every public institution.

(f) The flag should be displayed in or near every polling place on election days.

(g) The flag should be displayed during school days in or near every schoolhouse.

★ ★ ★ ★ ★   POSITION AND MANNER

OF DISPLAY

Sec. 3. That the flag, when carried in a procession with another flag or flags, should be either on the marching right; that is, the flag's own right, or, if there is a line of other flags, in front of the center of that line.

(a) The flag should not be displayed on a float in a parade except from a staff, or as provided in subsection (i).

(b) The flag should not be draped over the hood, top, sides, or back of a vehicle or of a railroad train or a boat. When the flag is displayed on a motorcar, the staff shall be fixed firmly to the chassis or clamped to the radiator cap.

(c) No other flag or pennant should be placed above or, if on the same level, to the right of the flag of the United States of America, except during church services conducted by naval chaplains at sea, when the church pennant may be flown above the flag during church services for the personnel of the Navy.

No person shall display the flag of the United Nations or any other national or international flag equal, above, or in a position of superior prominence or honor to, or in place of, the flag of the United States at any place within the United States or any Territory or possession thereof: *Provided,* That nothing in this section shall make unlawful the continuance of the practice heretofore followed of displaying the flag of the United Nations in a position of superior prominence or honor, and other national flags in positions of equal prominence or honor, with that of the flag of the United States at the headquarters of the United Nations.

(d) The flag of the United States of America, when

it is displayed with another flag against a wall from crossed staffs, should be on the right, the flag's own right, and its staff should be in front of the staff of the other flag.

(e) The flag of the United States of America should be at the center and at the highest point of the group when a number of flags of States or localities or pennants of societies are grouped and displayed from staffs.

(f) When flags of States, cities, or localities, or pennants of societies are flown on the same halyard with the flag of the United States, the latter should always be at the peak. When the flags are flown from adjacent staffs, the flag of the United States should be hoisted first and lowered last. No such flag or pennant may be placed above the flag of the United States or to the right of the flag of the United States.

(g) When flags of two or more nations are displayed, they are to be flown from separate staffs of the same height. The flags should be of approximately equal size. International usage forbids the display of the flag of one nation above that of another nation in time of peace.

(h) When the flag of the United States is displayed from a staff projecting horizontally or at an angle from the window sill, balcony, or front of a building, the union of the flag should be placed at the peak of the staff unless the flag is at half staff. When the flag is suspended over a sidewalk from a rope extending from a house to a pole at the edge of the sidewalk, the flag should be hoisted out, union first from the building.

(i) When the flag is displayed otherwise than by being

flown from a staff, it should be displayed flat, whether indoors or out, or so suspended that its folds fall as free as though the flag were staffed.

(j) When the flag is displayed over the middle of the street, it should be suspended vertically with the union to the north in an east and west street or to the east in a north and south street.

(k) When used on a speaker's platform, the flag, if displayed flat, should be displayed above and behind the speaker. When displayed from a staff in a church or public auditorium, if it is displayed in the chancel of a church, or on the speaker's platform in a public auditorium, the flag should occupy the position of honor and be placed at the clergyman's or speaker's right as he faces the congregation or audience. Any other flag so displayed in the chancel or on the platform should be placed at the clergyman's or speaker's left as he faces the congregation or audience. But when the flag is displayed from a staff in a church or public auditorium elsewhere than in the chancel or on the platform it shall be placed in the position of honor at the right of the congregation or audience as they face the chancel or platform. Any other flag so displayed should be placed on the left of the congregation or audience as they face the chancel or platform.

(l) The flag should form a distinctive feature of the ceremony of unveiling a statue or monument, but it should never be used as the covering for the statue or monument.

(m) The flag, when flown at half staff, should be first hoisted to the peak for an instant and then lowered to the half-staff position. The flag should be again raised to the peak before it is lowered for the day. By "half staff" is meant lowering the flag to one-half the distance between the top and bottom of the staff. Crepe streamers may be affixed to spear heads or flagstaffs in a parade only by order of the President of the United States.

(n) When the flag is used to cover a casket, it should be so placed that the union is at the head and over the left shoulder. The flag should not be lowered into the grave or allowed to touch the ground.

★ ★ ★ ★ ★ RESPECT FOR THE FLAG

Sec. 4. That no disrespect should be shown to the flag of the United States of America; the flag should not be dipped to any person or thing. Regimental colors, State flags, and organization or institutional flags are to be dipped as a mark of honor.

(a) The flag should never be displayed with the union down save as a signal of dire distress.

(b) The flag should never touch anything beneath it, such as the ground, the floor, water, or merchandise.

(c) The flag should never be carried flat or horizontally, but always aloft and free.

(d) The flag should never be used as drapery of any sort whatsoever, never festooned, drawn back, nor up, in folds, but always allowed to fall free. Bunting of blue, white, and red, always arranged with the blue above, the white in the middle, and the red below, should be used for covering a speaker's desk, draping the front of a platform, and for decoration in general.

(e) The flag should never be fastened, displayed,

used, or stored in such a manner as will permit it to be easily torn, soiled, or damaged in any way.

(f) The flag should never be used as a covering for a ceiling.

(g) The flag should never have placed upon it, nor on any part of it, nor attached to it any mark, insignia, letter, word, figure, design, picture, or drawing of any nature.

(h) The flag should never be used as a receptacle for receiving, holding, carrying, or delivering anything.

(i) The flag should never be used for advertising purposes in any manner whatsoever. It should not be embroidered on such articles as cushions or handkerchiefs and the like, printed or otherwise impressed on paper napkins or boxes or anything that is designed for temporary use and discard; or used as any portion of a costume or athletic uniform. Advertising signs should not be fastened to a staff or halyard from which the flag is flown.

(j) The flag, when it is in such condition that it is no longer a fitting emblem for display, should be destroyed in a dignified way, preferably by burning.

★ ★ ★ ★ ★ CONDUCT DURING HOISTING,
LOWERING, OR PASSING
OF FLAG

Sec. 5. That during the ceremony of hoisting or lowering the flag or when the flag is passing in a parade or in a review, all persons present should face the flag, stand at attention, and salute. Those present in uniform should render the military salute. When not in uniform, men should remove the headdress with the right hand holding it at the left shoulder, the hand being over the heart. Men without hats should salute in the same manner. Aliens should stand at attention. Women should salute by placing the right hand over the heart. The salute to the flag in the moving column should be rendered at the moment the flag passes.

★ ★ ★ ★ ★ CONDUCT DURING PLAYING OF
THE STAR-SPANGLED BANNER

Sec. 6. That when the national anthem is played and the flag is not displayed, all present should stand and face toward the music. Those in uniform should salute at the first note of the anthem, retaining this position until the last note. All others should stand at attention, men removing the headdress. When the flag is displayed, all present should face the flag and salute.

★ ★ ★ ★ ★ PLEDGE OF ALLEGIANCE
TO THE FLAG

Sec. 7. That the following is designated as the pledge of allegiance to the flag: "I pledge allegiance to the flag of the United States of America and to the Republic for which it stands, one Nation under God, indivisible, with liberty and justice for all." Such pledge should be rendered by standing with the right hand over the heart. However, civilians will always show full respect to the flag when the pledge is given by merely standing at attention, men removing the headdress. Persons in uniform shall render the military salute.

★ ★ ★ ★ ★ MODIFICATIONS BY THE
PRESIDENT

Sec. 8. Any rule or custom pertaining to the display of the flag of the United States of America, set forth herein, may be altered, modified, or repealed, or additional rules with respect thereto may be prescribed, by the Commander in Chief of the Army and Navy of the United States, whenever he deems it to be appropriate or desirable; and any such alteration or additional rule shall be set forth in a proclamation.

★ ★ ★ ★ ★ NOTES ON FLAG LAWS AND POINTS
OF ETIQUETTE

Penalties for Violations

The Federal flag code imposes no penalties for misuse of the national flag. Penalties are imposed by the individual states, each of which has its own flag laws. The federal government exercises control over flag matters only as they affect interstate commerce or as they apply to the District of Columbia.

District of Columbia Laws

In 1917 Congress passed a law prohibiting the mutilation of the flag and banning its use for advertising purposes in the District of Columbia.

Prohibition on Trademarks

The first Federal flag law in the nation's history was passed in 1905. It prohibited the use of the Stars and

Stripes in a registered trademark. In 1946 this law was amended to read that a trademark could not be registered if it "consists of or comprises the flag or coat of arms or other insignia of the United States or of any State or municipality, or of any foreign nation, or any simulation thereof."

Changes in Design of National Flag

The design of the Stars and Stripes can be altered only by an act of Congress, or presidential order. When Alaska statehood was assured in 1958, President Eisenhower appointed a flag committee of five members to arrange the 49 stars in the canton. A similar procedure was followed in designing the 50-starred flag.

Responsibility for Design of Federal Flags

Prior to 1947 this power was unofficially vested in the United States Navy. After the Unification Act of 1947 the responsibility for redesigning federal flags was given to the Heraldic Branch of the Quartermaster General's Office in the Department of the Army.

Display of Outdated Flags

Even though new stars may be added to the national flag it is not improper to display flags with the old number of stars.

Soiled and Worn Flags

Soiled flags may be renovated by either washing or dry cleaning. Worn-out flags should be destroyed by burning.

Display of Flag at Half-staff following Death of Certain Public Officials

On March 1, 1954, a proclamation by President Eisenhower established rules for flying the Stars and Stripes at half-mast as "a mark of respect" upon the death of major officials (and former officials) of the United States government. The flag should fly at half-mast for:

1. Thirty days from the day of death of a President or former President;
2. Ten days from the day of death of a vice-president, Chief Justice or retired Chief Justice of the United States, or a speaker of the House of Representatives;
3. From the day of death until interment for an associate justice of the Supreme Court, a member of the Cabinet, a former vice-president, or the secretaries of the Army, Navy, and Air Force;
4. On the day of death and on the following day for a United States senator, representative, territorial delegate, or resident commissioner of Puerto Rico—within the metropolitan area of the District of Columbia; on the day of death until interment within the state, congressional district, territory, or commonwealth. The latter provision also applies to the death of a governor of a state, territory, or possession.

★ ★ ★ ★ ★

★ ★ ★ ★ ★

★ ★ ★ ★ ★

APPENDIX ||||||||||||||||||||||||||||||||||||||||||

||||||||||||||||||||||||||||||||||||||||||||||||||||||||||||||||||||||||||

★ ★ ★ ★ ★   FAMOUS FIRSTS OF FLAGS
OF THE U.S.A.

1775, June 17: The first distinctive American flags to appear in battle are placed atop the defenses at Breed's Hill and Bunker Hill in the first full-scale engagement of the Revolutionary War; these flags, in their adaptations of the British red ensign, probably all bore a pine tree.

1775, Nov. 29: Pine-tree banners also serve as naval ensigns: the green-and-white flag of Captain John Manley's *Lee* flies over first American naval victory, the capture of the British brig *Nancy*.

1776, Jan. 1: The Grand Union, the first national flag of the embryonic United States, comes into being: it is hoisted at General George Washington's headquarters of the Continental Army in Cambridge, Mass.

1776, March: Grand Union Flag goes to sea for the first time: it is the ensign of the newly organized Continental Navy, commanded by Commodore Esek Hopkins, which sails out of Delaware Bay into the Atlantic Ocean.

1776, November: First foreign salute (11 guns) accorded American flag (the Grand Union) given by Fort Orange in Dutch West Indies.

1777, June 14: The nation's first flag law is passed when the design of the Stars and Stripes (13 stars and 13 stripes) is approved by Continental Congress as the first legally adopted national flag of the United States.

1777, Aug. 16: Stars and Stripes in the form of the so-called Bennington Flag marks first appearance of new banner in battle, near Bennington, Vt.

1777, Nov. 1: The first use of the Stars and Stripes as the American naval ensign occurs when John Paul Jones sails the *Ranger* out of Portsmouth, N.H., en route to France.

1778, Jan. 28: Fort Nassau, Bahama Islands, captured by American fleet, is scene of first raising of Stars and Stripes outside of the United States.

1778, Feb. 14: Stars and Stripes hoisted by John Paul Jones's *Ranger*, receives first recognition by a foreign power, a salute of nine guns by French fleet in Quiberon Bay on the south side of the Brittany peninsula.

1783, Feb. 4: Great Britain proclaims end of Revolutionary War; thus Stars and Stripes becomes legally recognized national flag of independent United States.

1787, Sept. 30–1790, Aug. 10: American flag first carried around the world, by Captain

Robert Gray sailing from Boston to Pacific Coast on the *Lady Washington* and from there westward to Boston again aboard the *Columbia.*

1795, May 1: In first change of original flag law passed in 1777, Congress creates flag of 15 stars and 15 stripes to give recognition to the first two states (Vermont and Kentucky) admitted to Union under the Constitution.

1812, May: Popular custom of public schools' flying national flag begins with first recorded raising of Stars and Stripes over a schoolhouse, at Colrain, Mass.

1814, Sept. 14: Name of "Star-Spangled Banner" given to national flag in song (later national anthem) written by Francis Scott Key in honor of defense of Fort McHenry, Baltimore, during British bombardment in War of 1812.

1818, July 4: Congress enacts third flag law effective this date; law establishes banner of 13 stripes and 20 stars, and fixes 13 stripes as permanent number in the flag; provision is made for automatically adding a new star for each new state admitted to the Union on the July 4 following the official granting of statehood.

1819, July 4: First star (for Illinois which became a state Dec. 3, 1818) added to flag under law of 1818; during next century and a half 29 more stars will be added without need for congressional action.

1824, March 17: Name of " Old Glory" given to national flag by William Driver, commander of

Charles Doggett, at Salem, Mass., when friends present him with finely made Stars and Stripes.

1834: United States Army authorizes artillery to carry Stars and Stripes as regimental color: the first legal use of national flag by military unit in the field.

1841: Use of Stars and Stripes as regimental color is extended to the infantry by Army regulations.

1861, June 14: Surge of patriotism during early days of Civil War leads to first observance of Flag Day, at Hartford, Conn. (date chosen is anniversary of nation's first flag law establishing the Stars and Stripes.)

1892: Pledge of Allegiance to the flag is written by James B. Upham and Francis Bellamy in effort to revive patriotic feelings on four hundredth anniversary of Columbus' discovery of America.

1905, Feb. 20: Increasing use of Stars and Stripes design for commercial purposes arouses opposition in Congress: registration of a trademark that "consists of or comprises the flag or coat of arms or other insignia of the United States" is prohibited by federal law.

1907: In absence of comprehensive federal legislation many states prohibited certain uses of national flag: constitutionality of state statutes penalizing desecration of Stars and Stripes upheld by United States Supreme Court.

1912, June 24: First official specifications of design in Stars and Stripes established by executive order of President William Howard Taft;

order prescribes exact placement and proportions of all design elements in flag.

1916, June 14: First Flag Day observed by presidential (Woodrow Wilson) proclamation which urges recognition of date Congress adopted the Stars and Stripes as national flag.

1923-1924: Flag conferences of many patriotic groups and individuals meet at Washington, D.C., and draw up a code prescribing proper display and usage of the national flag.

1942, Dec. 22: Congress adopts as federal law the flag code recommended by flag conference 18 years earlier.

1943: Following federal adoption of flag code many states had made pledge of allegiance to flag compulsory for school children; United States Supreme Court invalidates state laws requiring individuals to pledge allegiance to the flag.

1949, Aug. 3: President Harry S. Truman officially designates June 14 as Flag Day, thus giving formal approval to anniversary recognition accorded the Stars and Stripes on that date for some time previous.

1954, June 14: Congressional resolution adds phrase "under God" to flag pledge which had been incorporated into federal law as part of flag code in 1942.

1959, July 4: The 48-starred national flag, which served for forty-seven years (longer than any other Stars and Stripes), replaced by new emblem of of 49 stars commemorating admission of Alaska into the Union.

1959, Aug. 21: Design of 50-star flag authorized by President Dwight D. Eisenhower to give recognition to admission of Hawaii into the Union; this banner, the twenty-seventh Stars and Stripes, to come into being the following July 4.

1960, July 4: Flag with fiftieth star added is hoisted at 12:01 A.M. over Fort McHenry by presidential order; site selected to honor 1814 military victory celebrated in song by "The Star-Spangled Banner."

★ ★ ★ ★ ★ FLYING THE STARS AND
STRIPES AT NIGHT

The display of the flag of the United States at night is the subject of some confusion and misinformation. The actual number of places where the Stars and Stripes flies 24 hours a day is severely limited by two stipulations of the flag code (Public Law 829) Section 2 (a), which states: "It is the universal custom to display the flag only from sunrise to sunset. . . . However, the flag may be displayed at night upon special occasions when it is desired to produce a patriotic effect." The second restriction occurs in (c) of the same section: "The flag should not be displayed on days when the weather is inclement."

As a result of these restrictions there are only nine places in the United States where the Stars and Stripes flies around the clock. Three of these places have received specific legal authority; the other six take their authorization from established local custom which predates the 1942 enactment of the flag code or from an interpretation of the phrases "special occasions" and "to produce a patriotic effect" in the flag code itself. The United States Flag Foundation urges that the flag be illuminated if it is to be flown at night.

Fort McHenry, Baltimore, Md.

By Specific Legal Authority

(1) **Fort McHenry National Monument and Historic Shrine, Baltimore, Md.** Proclamation by President Harry S. Truman on July 2, 1948: "As a perpetual symbol of our patriotism, the flag of the United States shall hereafter be displayed at Fort McHenry National Monument and Historic Shrine at all times

Appendix ★ 211

during the day and night, except when the weather is inclement." (As interpreted by park officials the weather has not interfered with the continuous display of the flag.) During the stout defense of this fort during the War of 1812 the national flag was never lowered. Thus it seemed particularly appropriate to authorize continued display of the Stars and Stripes, in peace as well as war.

Flag House, Baltimore, Md.

(2) **Flag House Square, Baltimore, Md.** Public Law 319, approved March 26, 1954: "To permit the flying of the flag of the United States for twenty-four hours of each day in Flag House Square." Here again the Stars and Stripes is displayed regardless of weather. Also flown around the clock in Flag House Square is a replica of the 15-starred, 15-striped flag of the War of 1812, famed as the "Star-Spangled Banner."

Flag House is the former home of Mary Young Pickersgill, who made the flag Francis Scott Key saw flying over Fort McHenry in "the dawn's early light" of September 14, 1814.

(3) **Marine Corps Memorial (Iwo Jima Statue), Arlington, Va.** Proclamation by President John F. Kennedy on June 14, 1961: "Whereas the raising of the American flag during that battle [Iwo Jima] over Mt. Suribachi on February 23, 1945, symbolizes the courage and valor of the American fighting forces in World War II. . . [I] proclaim that the flag of the United States of America shall hereafter be displayed at the United States Marine Corps Memorial in Arlington, Virginia, at all times during the day and night except when the weather is inclement." The memorial illustrates in statue form the historic Iwo Jima flag raising. (Picture, p. 171.)

By Local Custom or Law Interpretation

(1) **Taos, New Mexico.** This is the site of the longest continuous display of the Stars and Stripes. In 1861 Civil War fighting, Confederate bands invaded the city on several occasions, each time cutting down the national flag flying in the town plaza. An enraged Union Army captain, Smith H. Simpson, finally nailed the flag to a tall cottonwood pole he erected in the plaza. With the aid of frontier scout Kit Carson and other Union sympathizers, Simpson successfully defied all further attempts to haul down the Stars and Stripes, day or night. Proud of this stubborn resistance, the town of Taos has displayed the national flag continuously in its plaza since that time.

Mount Olivet Cemetery, Frederick, Md.

(2) **Mount Olivet Cemetery, Frederick, Md.** Here the national flag flies over the grave of Francis Scott Key 24 hours a day, regardless of the weather. This custom began sometime before World War I in honor of one of Maryland's premier citizens, the composer of "The Star-Spangled Banner."

(3) **United States Capitol, Washington, D.C.** A congressional act of 1894 provided for the daily hoisting of the national flag over both the east and west

fronts of the center of the Capitol. The custom of keeping both these flags flying continuously began as a result of popular patriotic requests during World War I. (Flags fly over the Senate and House wings of the Capitol only when those legislative bodies are in session.)

(4) **Worcester War Memorial, Worcester, Mass.** The flag of the United States has been flying day and night at this memorial in Lincoln Square since November 11, 1933. Since the memorial is dedicated to the honor of the war dead, it seemed appropriate to display the Stars and Stripes around the clock as a further tribute.

Brown Rocks, Deadwood, S.D.

(5) **Deadwood, S.D**. During World War I this city in the Black Hills began flying the Stars and Stripes around the clock from picturesque Brown Rocks near the city. After the war the custom was abandoned. But with the attack on Pearl Harbor December 7, 1941, and a new national crisis at hand (World War II), city officials rehoisted the flag. It has been kept flying day and night since that time.

(6) **Francis Scott Key Birthplace, Terra Rubra Farm, Keymar, Md.** A stone monument marks the site of Key's birthplace on a farm in Carroll County. The Stars and Stripes atop this monument has flown 24 hours a day since May 30, 1949, when it was hoisted in Memorial Day ceremonies honoring the composer of the national anthem. The flag is maintained by the Kiwanis Club of Westminster.

Contrary to some reports the national flag is not displayed at night atop Pikes Peak, Colo; at the Custer Battlefield National Monument, Crow Agency, Mont.; Independence National Historical Park, Philadelphia; Tomb of the Unknown Soldier, Arlington National Cemetery, Va.; Colton, Calif. (although the Stars and Stripes did fly day and night atop nearby Mt. Slover from 1917 to 1952—a mining excavation destroyed flagsite).

★ ★ ★ ★ ★   MILITARY USE OF STARS
AND STRIPES
In each of the armed services of the United States the national flag receives special respect and performs specific functions.

In the Army. Army Regulations 840-10 prescribe that the flag of the United States "will be displayed at all Army installations [usually from reveille to retreat]. It also will be displayed at one seacoast or lake fort, or a group of forts within sight of each other at the beginning of and during an action in which the forts may be engaged, whether by day or night. Not more than one flag of the United States will be flown at one time at any Army installation except as may be specially authorized by Headquarters, Department of the Army. . . ." In the field the national flag is displayed in front of the commanding officer's headquarters (when practicable).

An Army garrison flag measures 20 feet hoist by 38 feet fly. A post flag is exactly one half as large; a storm flag is one-half the size of the post flag. The fringed and tasseled national color, used for ceremonial occasions, takes the same size as the organization flag or color with which it is displayed.

The United States Army flag is carried or displayed only in conjunction with and subordinate to the national flag. When the flags of other armed services are present the order of precedence is Army, Marine Corps, Navy, and Air Force.

In the presence of the United Nations flag, the Army displays the national flag (of the same size and at the same level) in the position of honor on the right (observer's left). When both flags are carried by troops, the United Nations flag is on the marching left of the United States flag.

In the Navy. In addition to the Stars and Stripes, called the national ensign, the United States Navy flies a flag bearing the stars alone on a blue field, called the

Union Jack; a long, slim banner bearing seven stars with one red and one white stripe, called the commission pennant; and the personal flag or command pennant of an officer of the Navy. The distinctive mark of a ship in commission is the display of either a personal flag (command pennant) or a commission pennant. This pennant is displayed night and day at the after masthead, or in a mastless ship, from the loftiest hoist.

When at anchor or in port (not under way) the ensign is displayed from the flagstaff at the stern and the jack from the jackstaff at the bow from 0800 until sunset. At sea the ensign flies from the gaff during daylight. The headquarters of shore installations displays the ensign from 0800 to sunset. Other customs on land are much the same as those followed by the Army.

Navy regulations require that a vessel dip its ensign only in return for a complimentary dip from a ship registered by a formally recognized nation. On occasions of dressing a ship, a national ensign is displayed from each masthead.

Of special interest is the display of the ensign aboard the USS *Arizona*. This ship, sunk in the attack on Pearl Harbor, December 7, 1941, is considered to be still "in commission" with the 1,102 men entombed aboard her officially buried at sea. Each day a color guard raises the Stars and Stripes at 0800 and lowers it at sunset.

In the Marine Corps. A part of the Department of the Navy, the Marine Corps performs the official honors to the national flag at home, at United States bases overseas, and at American embassies in foreign lands. Marine flag customs and traditions are similar to those of the

Army and Navy. A Marine patrol carried out the historic hoisting of the United States flag atop Mount Suribachi on Iwo Jima in World War II.

In the Coast Guard. Although the Coast Guard is a component of the Department of the Treasury it is usually assigned to the Navy in wartime. It flies a national ensign, Union Jack, Coast Guard ensign, and personal flag, command pennant, or commission pennant. Regulations governing the display of the Stars and Stripes are similar to those in use in the Navy.

In the Air Force. Because it was part of the United States Army until 1947, Air Force regulations concerning the display of the national flag are similar to those of the older service. The Stars and Stripes is flown from Air Force bases in the United States and abroad during daylight hours.

INDEX